Also by

Sheila Stephens

Walking With the Flowers;
Weekly Quiet Time Meditations
For a Woman's Busy Life

Adventures in Writing 101
A Backpack of Tools for the Starry Path
Of Creative Writing

available at
Flowers of the Spirit.com

Sheila Stephens also Appears in:

Chocolate for a Woman's Soul II
Chocolate for a Woman's Blessings
Chocolate for a Woman's Courage
Chocolate for a Woman's Dreams
Chocolate for a Teen's Soul
Chocolate for a Teen's Spirit
Chocolate for a Lover's Heart
By Kay Allenbaugh

And

Seasoned with Words
By The Oregon Writers Colony

We all have good intentions, but in this busy
day and age, our promises to pray for friends,
family, and even ourselves are often left by the wayside.
Here's not only an easy, but a divinely delicious way
to recapture the magic of prayer time.
Just pour yourself a luxurious cup of tea,
hold its beauty in your hands,
and let the Higher Spirit of Love
lift the vibrations of your day.

The Art of Prayer
& Tea & Thee

*A New Way to Find a Moment to Pray
In the Midst of Our Busy Days*

Sheila Stephens

It's a Girl Friend's Way!

Flowers of the Spirit LLC
SHERWOOD, OREGON
WEB-STORE: Flowers of the Spirit.com

Published and distributed in the United States of America by
Flowers of the Spirit LLC, P. O. Box 1028
Sherwood, OR 97140
FAX: (503) 925-8564
WEB-STORE: Flowers of the Spirit.com

Cover Design & Photograph, Sheila Stephens

ISBN 0-9761022-0-X

LCCN 2004096780

Flowers of the Spirit™
Prayer & Tea & Thee™

Visit our WEB-STORE at www.FlowersOfTheSpirit.com
For books, fun workshops, and gifts to renew your spirit and
inspire your creativity.
Ask for a Free e-newsletter
And complimentary copy of "The Teatime Prayer"

Volume discounts for Groups, Fundraisers, and Individuals
desiring Quantity Purchases. Please see back of book or web-
store for ordering information.

To my wonderful husband, Allen,
And our two fine & caring sons, Jim & Julian

❤

because your love
has changed my life

- Contents -

Part I - The Art of Preparing Our Hearts

1. It's a Girl Friend's Way   1
   Deciding to Participate.

2. Surrounding Yourself With Your Favorite Things   7
   Setting the Stage for Something Special.

3. Put Your Feet Up & Your Worries Down   15
   The Sweetness of Surrendering to Something Higher.

4. Filling Up Your Cup   25
   Finding Abundance.

Part II - The Art of Receiving & Renewal

5. Letting Your Tea Steep   35
   Merging with the Divine.

6. A Sip of Warmth that Spreads through You   41
   Receiving Comfort - Body, Mind & Spirit Style.

7. There's a Reason a Teacup has a Handle!   47
   Getting a Grip on Strong Emotions.

8. Raising Your Teacup; Raising Your Vibration   53
   Attuning to a Higher Vision.

9. Enjoying High Tea - a Serving of Rich Blessings   61
   Honoring Abundance - by Using It in Your Life.

10. The Clink of Fine China   71
    Using a Delicate Sound to Stay Centered & Aware.

Part III - The Art of Activating Love's Intentions

11. Sip-by-Sip, Step-by-Step Miracles   79
    Sacred Co-Creating.

12. Even on the Shelf, the Teacup Talks   85
    Finding Lovely Reminders.

13. A Bubblebath for the Spirit!   95
    How the Comfort of Beauty's Ways
    Helps Your Spirit Luxuriate.

14. Deciding Serenity Isn't Such a "Little Thing"!   103
    Appreciating.

15. Teatime Is Anytime, Anywhere –
    Thank Goodness!   111
    Committing to Everyday Magic.

Part IV - Ceremony Remembrance Poem

Use this prayer-poem to walk yourself through the PRAYER &
TEA & THEE™ Ceremony anytime you want a quick reminder
of the steps –

"A Teatime Prayer"   *122*

- A Thank You Gift -

In celebration of the Circle of Love ignited
by each good-hearted person who prays, a
complimentary gift copy of *"A Teatime Prayer"*
is available over the Internet for you and your
friends at . . .
FlowersOfTheSpirit.com

Part I:

The Art of Preparing

Our Hearts

It's a Girl Friend's Way

Deciding to Participate, Deciding to Care.

As I look around the long table, I'm impressed, for so many good people come to a workshop based on the Art of Prayer. The tea is a bonus for them, I'm sure, but to me, they're the bonus. Their good hearts begin a process that goes far beyond the crisp white tablecloth I've laid out, the delicate touches of lace, and the gold-edged teacups that clink the way fine china does. But ah-h, we do enjoy these lovely things - fine china and the like - and it's fun to see how our smiles return as we accept a bit of luxury amidst our busy days.

A Girl Friend's Way, a Bridge of Love

It's definitely a Girl Friend's way! It is such a woman's way to reach out and care for her friends - by building a bridge of Love to them; by taking time to pray for them, even as our own days brim with a veritable laundry basket of demands to be met. That's how this pleasurable

Tea Ceremony began for me: with a desire to keep a promise. A heartfelt promise to pray for a friend. But, just as you may find, after I'd willingly made a promise to pray for a friend, my time seemed to fill with a cacophony of cell phones ringing, work that must be done, and chores that wouldn't wait. Where in the world would I find time to keep my promise, I asked myself, and be the kind of friend I most wanted to be?

That's When the Fun Began . . .

To my surprise, the fun began almost immediately. Sometimes the answers to our own prayers are only moments away. Here I was, still on the phone to my friend, Amanda, wondering how in the world I was going to keep my promise, and take time to pray for her the way I wanted to, when I started receiving an interesting answer. My eyes fell upon a treasured yellow and gold antique teacup on the cherry bookcase nearby.

"Yes, Amanda, even when it's hectic, I will be able to keep my word and pray for you. In fact, I'm going to use something fun to remind me to pray when I get busy and might forget." I grinned at the thought of it. "Every time I look at my teacup, I'll use it to remind me to pray. In fact . . . any teacup I see can remind me!"

"Ah ha!" "What fun!" These were some of the expressions that issued forth from two well-intentioned women who really wanted to keep some very important promises. Amanda and I were so relieved to find such a short and sweet, even whimsical way to remind us both to pray, that we felt giddy with relief.

Could it be this easy, I wondered? Higher Spirit's answer was - Yes, it could be *even easier.* In fact, every time *I had a cup of tea,* I could raise my teacup, and raise my vibrations. As I relaxed and enjoyed each warm sip, I could align with God's great Love, and pray for a friend.

My Girl Friend's heart was smiling. What a natural way to pray for a friend - over a comforting cup of tea!

What a Way to Keep a Promise!

What a beautiful way to take time to pray, I thought! And as soon as I shared this inspiration, Amanda and I both knew we'd found something special. Thank You, I said to Spirit later, as I so easily lifted a cup of tea, and even in the middle of my hectic evening, kept my promise - and took some loving time to pray for a friend.

What a bounty I suddenly found as I held a new kind of beauty in my hands. Helping me pray for my friend were plenty of my own friends: delicate gold-rimmed teacups; dainty pink and blue floral teacups; teacups with rose printed porcelain; teacups with lush peonies and fresh white daisies; and teacups that were priceless because they were gifts from my mom and my friends. This was more than a woman could hope for!

But there was more. Sometimes I wanted a good ol' mug. Like the burgundy one from the trip to the mountains of Montana. And the soft white one from the shores of the

Coast. And the deep midnight blue glass one with dream-words brushed in gold from one of my favorite writers. Ah-h, what a way to keep a promise, I thought. The only thing missing? This easy system of finding a moment to pray - even when there's not one - begged to be shared.

A Whole New Kind of Tea Ceremony!

One of the cool things about Spirit is all the wealth that arrives on the wings of an inspired Gift. Every time I thought about this answer to prayer - in the form of sipping tea! - I wanted to share it. Sheer happiness caught me in its updraft and I began sharing the wealth with friends right away. In the days and weeks that followed, I continued to receive a graceful stream of easy but important steps that could be called: a Tea Ceremony. A whole new kind of Tea Ceremony. It was similar to the Japanese Tea Ceremony, in that it was a ceremony that cherished the time spent in steps toward peaceful centering. But this ceremony was uniquely American, designed for busy women everywhere. It definitely wanted to be immediately accessible and refreshingly simple, with each step tending to the opening of our hearts - so each step could tend us as we sought to tend others.

As I've stepped into this Gift that came, almost unbidden, in answer to my own prayer, I've had the most fun giving *The Art of PRAYER & TEA & THEE*™ Workshops. Whether we've had fine linens and china teacups, or a basic table and casual mugs (or even coffee, tea, or hot chocolate!), we've all had our cups filled up with a megawatt voltage of Love as we proceeded to practice a new and thankfully easy way of keeping our cherished promise. To pray for another. To build a bridge of Love between friends. And in the process, to take ourselves into that much-longed-for place where the storm stops, the cell phones quiet, and our hearts find their way home again.

This is the joy that is so much fun to share. A Tea Ceremony that asks us to put our feet up and our worries down, so we might receive all the wealth that arrives on the wings of an inspired Gift. And in so doing, be naturally caught in the buoyant updraft of Love.

Sharing a Cup of Tea, a Gift from the Heart

Definitely, it is a woman's way: deciding to partici-pate - and open our hearts in a manner that allows the flow-ers of care and hope bloom for another person. And as we give to another, to be ineffably changed because of it. But in my workshops both men and women brought their generous hearts to the process, using what we all innately possess: a wonderful feminine nature that helps us open and receive inspiration, and a dynamic masculine nature that helps us activate these good ideas and put them into practice right here - in our real lives.

The results have been wildly re-energizing. Smiles, laughter, the warm buzz of excitement. Such is the power of prayer that in the process of taking time for another, we always benefit, too! So as we shared our cups of tea and prayed for a friend, we realized Spirit wanted to share a cup of tea with us and meet our own needs as well, oftentimes before we proceeded another step.

What do you need? Spirit would say. *A bit of rest? And a little luxurious tending?*

For the good people in my workshops, and for me, the answer to this was a whole-hearted "Yes!" But you don't need to go to a workshop to enjoy this life-giving process. Whether you take a short, even 2-minute break, or you spend a bit longer, this Prayer & Tea & Thee Ceremony is at your fingertips. A warm, delicious blessing any time you need it.

Fortunately, it's so easy, and so fun, to begin. Amazingly, it starts by helping us re-cultivate a delightful sense of *Play!*

Surrounding Yourself With Your Favorite Things

Setting the Stage for Something Special.

It's fun to think of entering the act of prayer as a playful thing, for no matter how we honestly want to pray, we sometimes mistakenly think that prayer time is just work - another thing on our already-too-long To Do List. But the first step in our Tea workshops is something very personal and always enjoyable: we choose our cup. Our favorite cup. Sounds like a simple thing, and it is, because the first thing Spirit is doing is simplifying our life. There's a lot of charm in setting all the chatter of our mind aside, much less our endless reams of responsibilities - and turning our attention instead to something like choosing our teacup. But there's also a great deal of power in it.

What Is It That You Bring to the Table?

As we start relaxing by focusing on only one question, instead of twenty, we make a conscious and powerful step of joy. To choose that which feels special. To choose that which feels right to us that day. In many ways, it's like a fun shopping trip. Whether you're choosing your favorite new item of clothing, or a new fishing pole, it's a great feeling to take your own needs into consideration and have the pleasure of selecting what's right for you.

This was a great surprise for a very nice man in one of my recent workshops. Recently retired, Don felt amazed by all the choices he now had to orchestrate his own day - choices he hadn't had before. The fact that Don could choose a cobalt blue cup that reminded him of the ocean, rather than the drab one he usually used, was something he hadn't thought about before. "I already enjoy my prayer time," Don said. "The beauty of the out-of-doors, the backyard where I sit to listen to the birds sing. But adding my own special cup - one that reflects who I am - now that really feels good."

I loved watching Don's face when he spoke about it - so much like the sun rising, or the kid-like joy of finding the perfect fishing pole. That's what Spirit wants for us in this wonderful, playful stage. To simply align with what we love, and bring it to the table.

The Beautiful Spirit of Who We Are

Our gifts to Spirit are many, but in this stage, it is a disarmingly loving gift to us, because Spirit knows that when we bring a cup we love to the table, we are bringing the cup of who we are. And that is the greatest gift to Spirit. Amazingly - the very greatest.

In this stage, I am now always humbled and overwhelmed - now positively! - by how much God loves me.

Appreciative tears sincerely spring to my eyes as I realize this is all that is required. Our presence. Our true and authentic presence. And now I realize, too, how much God must miss us when we don't share our presence with Him. When we get so busy that we don't bring the cup of who we are to the table, and share our conversations with Him.

In a new way now, those of us at the workshop table stand up and choose the cup for our tea. With joy and a feeling of being unconditionally loved, we see which cup reflects our spirit, and even how we feel today.

Bringing Our Here-&-Now-Selves to the Table

Have you ever felt that you loved one cup one day - maybe that splendid yellow sunflower mug - and then the next day, it had to be something totally different? Maybe the delicate porcelain cup with rose buds and scalloped gold trim? I think God smiles when we understand that today we feel different, for He not only loves us, but He wants us to bring our here-and-now, whatever-you're-in-the-middle-of selves to the table.

By doing so, we begin letting God in to help us with the real stuff that needs to be fixed in the middle of our real lives. We begin a beautiful path of partnering with Spirit (something we'll talk a lot about throughout this book). At first we may think choosing a cup is a simple and an insignificant thing, but when we let it reflect the spirit of who we are, and where we are today, we understand that it is a very special thing: it is our first offering to God. It is the beauty of who we are. Warts and worries. Hopes and fears. Triumphs and tears. And yes, amazingly, that is the gift God has been waiting for

.

Setting the Stage for Something Special

For this reason, it's a pleasure of the spirit to set the stage for something special. In this easy but artful process, we not only bring the beauty of who we are, right here, right now, to the table, but the act itself shows we are consciously making a choice: a beautiful choice to open and receive. The process of setting the stage still wants to be a fun one though. Very simple and manageable - so we'll look back later and remember how much we enjoyed it. So we'll do it often.

So what does "special" mean to you - today? What cup would you choose? Or what kind of tea would you like? And what other small item might you enjoy beside you, to set the stage and put your heart in gear? Sometimes in workshops, I'll bring a small piece of lace, not more than twelve inches long, but something I totally love. Then I'll put a pretty teacup on it, along with a small gold or silver stirring spoon. Not a regular teaspoon, but one of the petite variety. Specially chosen. Favorites include memory-filled ones from the Portland Rose Garden; the fabulous Butchart Gardens in Victoria, B.C.; and a quaint antique store my husband and I found in New Orleans. I'm already feeling better just thinking about them!

These few "special things" are so easy to put together, you can even take them traveling. You can always fit a teaspoon or a piece of lace (or a favorite napkin) into some luggage - and most hotels have a coffee cup if you don't want to pack that.

There are so many ways to set the stage for something special, so it's fun to practice a bit of whimsy, and pick something different that echoes your current mood and needs. Some days I realize the delicate teacup that calls to me reflects the fact that I'm *feeling* delicate. And in this way, it helps me. For honoring who we are and how we are today helps us begin to heal, so we might then be of service to others. In a beautiful way, we are the cup, the chalice, and it is our job to let ourselves be filled with Love, be healed by Love, and then to let Love's presence overflow our cup - into the lives of others.

So some days I happily pick up the delicate cup, and feel relieved to cherish my delicate self. Oh, how good it feels. And other days, I pick up a bright bold mug that holds passions and dreams that have been longing to be heard. What a relief that is, too - to know that all of me has room at the table with God. And each choice makes Him smile.

The Choice Is the Thing

Why is God smiling? One reason must be that we're finally making choices. We're making choices to bring ourselves to the table, sip a cup of tea, and be ourselves in a spiritual way. For we've been "being ourselves," and that is easy enough - to be ourselves without really thinking, by just reacting to events and demands within our day. But to make a choice to be ourselves in a spiritual way is quite another thing. To take a breather and enter a joyful quiet time, where Higher Spirit's guidance can fill us, meet our needs, and lift us up - that is quite an extraordinary thing.

With the simple choice of selecting our cup, or the kind of tea (or coffee), or setting the stage with a spoon or lace, or a chair out by the birds, we say who we are in a very different way. In the most beautiful of ways, we're saying - *I am, therefore I pray.*

And I am beautiful.

And I am of the Spirit.

As we hold the cup of who we are in our hands this way, we realize that whether we come in a state of delicacy or one of high energy creativity, we are the jubilant cup - we are the *Offering that Spirit longs to receive,* in this now personal place of prayer. By selecting a cup that expresses who we are this moment, this day, we have done just that, we've made our prayer time personal.

It doesn't take long to start this sacred process of fun reconnecting, for after doing this for some time, I've noticed the change it makes in me - and in the energy around me. Now, as my fingertips close around the handle of the cup I've chosen, I notice as quickly as night follows day, *I've already started receiving those megawatt volts of Love!* The Love that was always there, just waiting for my slightest commitment - to bring such awesome and welcome comfort to all the corners of my days.

As Spirit's sunny thunderbolts of Love gently stream through the cup handle and into my heart, I know that not only this cup, but *this experience* is definitely one of my favorite things!

Put Your Feet Up
& Your Worries Down

The Sweetness of Surrendering to Something Higher.

After we've selected our teacup, it's time for some serious and well-earned pampering. There are many fine feelings in life, and one of the sweetest is the feeling we get when we put our feet up and set our worries down. Whether you're in a place where you can find a comfy chair and ottoman, or just imagine yourself in one, it's so healthy to take this much-needed breather, and luxuriate by surrendering all those heavy worries to Spirit.

As we put our feet up (I can almost hear the sighs!) and imagine ourselves taking our heavy backpack of problems off our shoulders and putting it down beside us instead, it's good to remember we are not giving up nor giving in. Instead, we are very wisely deciding to share the load. I say "very wisely," for how often we forget to do just that! "Oh yeah," we lightheartedly smack ourselves in the forehead as we collapse in a heap at the end of the day, "I can share this load I've got! This bundle that definitely feels too heavy!"

We might even ask ourselves, "Why were we carrying it anyway?"

"Well, someone has to," might come the answer, for society has taught us well the ways to carry our responsibilities. In fact, I love the people who come to prayer workshops for they are wonderfully responsible, caring people. But Spirit now asks us to think about what being Responsible really means, and more deeply consider the RESPONSIVE part in the word Responsible. Maybe it's time to ask ourselves what - or who - we're being responsive to? And if we're burnt out, over-tasked and overburdened, maybe we're not being responsive to Higher Spirit and how He wants to care for us, so we can later serve others again, but from a beautiful, more balanced place.

"But how do we get there?" you ask. "How do we get to that more balanced place?"

Put Your Feet Up & Your Worries Down

Isn't it a huge relief to think about putting your feet up and your worries down? To stop being overly responsible for a moment, and answer your spirit's cry? I'm so glad this is the next step in the Tea Ceremony, for we yearn to take a break for a reason. My friend, Jason, remembers having High Tea in Canada as a boy. He was very affected by it, and loved the fact that everyone would stop to take a breather in the afternoon - when it wasn't even lunch time - and would actually *plan* to do so. In some real and vital way, it met his spirit's needs. (Jason later became a counselor, listening to his own needs and teaching others to listen to theirs.)

Our spirit does have needs, of course, but we're not always good at listening to those needs. I love the way my cat does it though. Sadie flops on the floor directly in front of me and straightforwardly asks me to meet her needs - *scratch me here; pet me; soothe me!* Oh, that we could be more like her, in touch with our bodies and the clues they offer us about how we need some tending. In the course of our day, our spirit is receiving just that, its own kind of miracle-in-waiting type of guidance through the powerful signals of our mind and our body. Does your mind feel as if it's on overload, filled with negatives, too exhausted to be the positive, light-filled person you were this morning? Or does your body feel weighted down, or your chest tense, unable to take a full, deep breath? In all the hubbub of keeping up with life's demands, does it feel as though you've forgotten how to dance?

"You bet!" most of us would say at some point in our day or week. "This is a part of life!" And indeed it is, but it's not all of life. In fact, it's a signal to take a new direction, choose your favorite teacup, and put your feet up and your worries down. Do so, and you may find your cat or pet at your side, contentedly taking a spirit break with you.

We Don't Have To Do It Alone!

All too often, most of us think we have to fly solo and figure our way through a problem - by ourselves. Be responsible. Work hard at it. But that's not always the solution. That's not always Spirit's way. That backpack of worries on

your shoulder? Isn't it a relief to know that Spirit wants it?
In fact, Spirit is asking for it!

It's an incredible thing to remember this backpack
of worries is meant to be shared. For every busy mom who
carries the concerns about her family and even the challenge
of building a nurturing home on her shoulders, what a relief
it is to know you're meant to sit down at regular intervals in
the day - and share the challenges with God. For every person who goes to work and deals with all kinds of people and
crazy traffic to boot, isn't it a welcome relief to know you
don't need to keep on working and working constantly, but
that your own needs are important, too? What a welcome
relief to know all this bundle of stress, or triumphs and
concerns can be set down - and shared by a compassionate
God who sees our every challenge and every need. And that
setting this heavy backpack down can be as easy as putting
our feet up, and picking up a soothing cup of tea instead?

One reason I love this new kind of Tea Ceremony is I
now know I can be successful, that even on evenings when I'm
really wiped out, I can sit down, and sip a cup of tea. How, even
if I spend only a short amount of time, it can change my consciousness. And I can suddenly pray. Before this, I often did
the same thing and took a break for tea, but now it's imbued
with a new spirit, a new meaning. Even a new anticipation.

Making Space for God In All of This

What crystallizes our decision and allows us to put
our feet up and take the life-giving kind of breather our

body is requesting? In all of this, this stuff we call life, I ask myself if I am making room for God? Sometimes it hits me over the head that I am not. I "think" I'm being very responsible, filling my days up with all kinds of good deeds. And it seems I never do get to the end of my list. In fact, all too often I'm falling into that chair, exhausted and depleted by trying to be a good person. But what is God's definition of a good person?

Is it a person who works so hard, they are separate from Him? Is it really a person who doesn't allow themselves to rest and recuperate - and replenish the very spirit that holds God's love? And is this really how we help our family or friends - by not even having time to pray for them? In essence, is everything accomplished on the physical plane of doing, doing, doing, or is there another spiritual plane that wants to also be used, so it might affect the very outcomes we so good-heartedly seek?

When we put the heavy backpack of our worries down, we practice a conscious spiritual act. In a symbolic way, we're saying that we are not alone. And what a huge relief it is to REMEMBER this! The best of us can forget, and go on about our life as if we were putting out fires instead of entering into an act of sacred co-creation. No, we are not alone, and leaving room for God to work within ourselves and our lives brings the real power and joy of creation to it.

I once had a dream. In my real life I was tackling a very difficult challenge, one that probably would hit 10 on the scale of 1 to 10 of difficulty. But it was interesting, in the dream I was told *to stop trying so hard.* Not only did my excess striving get in God's way, for He was doing part of it, but it showed a lack of confidence! Wow! Did that impact me. For in every good-hearted person, there is a Doer inside us that thinks we must do our part, and continued action is the key. But God was saying something else. *Leave me room,* He was saying, *and remember the act is one of co-creation. This is a partnership. When you do too much, you don't give me the room I need to do my part!*

So when we set our worries down, we are lovingly acknowledging God, and giving Him room to move within our lives. It's so good to remember this, because each time a new worry comes up, this pattern of doing it alone, without the comfort of Higher Spirit's participation, can repeat itself. Just this weekend we planted a big, beautiful 18-foot Birch tree in our backyard. The next morning, my husband pointed out to me how the branches were wilting slightly - and I began - Yes! - to worry!

At some point I remembered this part of the Tea Ceremony, humorously smacked myself lightly on the forehead again!, and consciously put my worries down. And yes, it was still a bit hard to do, for the habit is so ingrained in us! But as I set that bundle of worry down, it allowed me to start imagining Love flowing into that tree. And I began imagining how happily it would grace our yard for years to come. Now I was in God's creative flow, and it suddenly felt much better.

Moving Beyond the Confines of Worry

Sometimes we carry our burdens and worries around because we don't want to think about them. Yet they still are there, a silent but heavy yoke upon our shoulders. "But I'm afraid to start listing all the negatives," you say. "They're overwhelming." As you can see from the story above, I can certainly identify with that. Now here we are, feeling stressed out and negative, and you're being asked to let it all hang out and, in essence, be negative. So the tip here is to set our worries down - while we put our feet up. Letting go of our worries, into the arms of something Higher is an art form that's worth the practicing, but it is a new way of thinking. Our ego-mind sees what it perceives as limitations and lack of possibilities about those precious worries - so it can stop us in our tracks.

But God sees such opportunities and expansive possibilities - and the new wisdom we can gain as we learn from Him. He sees that in good things we can learn from Him. And He sees that in challenges we can learn from Him. And He wants to fill our lives with such Grace, so that in both good times and bad times, we can find His gift of Balance - and feel a personal inner Peace.

After all, the most wonderful kind of mother, the kind we want to be around is not a worried one, but a Peaceful one. And the most powerful husband is not a stressed-out husband, but a balanced, Peace-filled husband. And the best friend to have is the kind who knows how to find his or her center, and shares that loving Peace and calm joy with you.

The people who are like this know one big secret:
they don't do it all by themselves. They don't solve life's
problems all alone. Instead they honestly and consistently
bring their daily stress, their worries and concerns into
their refreshment time - and let Higher Spirit soothe them,
heal them, and then inspire them.

Transforming Worries into Prayers

It is in this place of peace, when we ourselves are
healed and in balance that we can pray effectively for others. So as you put your feet up and your worries down, know
that you're in the process of opening up this generous path
of prayer and healing for your friends and family, too. Each
step we take toward our own peacefulness lets in the Light of
Love for those we so deeply care about. But each step of
prayer, whether for ourselves or for others, needs to begin
with honesty.

It's OK here to speak the honest truth of what you're
feeling or confronting. Naming it has its own relief. But it
is also here that we no longer have to hold it alone. Thank
goodness God is there to not only share the load, but take the
biggest part of it!

As we give it to God, something magical happens. We
breathe again. Sunlight evaporates the boundaries of our
shortsightedness. And Love moves with wings that had been
previously invisible to us.

Being truthful leads us to new truth. New compassion. New wisdoms. New ideas. As we give God our honest

load, we find - much to our delight - that along the way the potential creative spirit, the real offering of who we are, has been activated! We're no longer just a passive part of the problem. Now, as we participate and receive, we become part of the Light-filled possibilities and loving solutions! We might even find ourselves praying for trees!

But would all the new ideas and expansive feelings that flow forth more naturally now have been possible without bringing our real problems into the equation? No, for just as God wants us to make room for Him, He needs us to make room for ourselves, for our real fears and worries, because *in order to receive - we must release.* To do so honestly is to give the greatest compliment to God, for it is then we give Him access to our heart and let Him do His work. And in this sweet surrender we find the finest form of pampering. *Set your worries down, and let me bring you Peace.*

What a relief it is - to sit in a big old chair where our spirit's real needs are met. It feels so good to see our backpack of worries, no longer on our shoulders, but sitting instead beside us at our feet. In our workshops, we shed yet another stress as we take a moment to robustly give up the guilt we might have felt for taking a breather, knowing now that we're making room for God each time we pick up our teacup - and either physically or symbolically, put up our feet!

Filling Up Your Cup

Finding Abundance.

There's always an air of expectancy for me when bubbling hot water pours exuberantly into my own special teacup. As the steam rises and its happy spirit playfully threatens to fog up my glasses, I feel like a little girl again, experiencing a small bit of magic in the middle of my every-day world.

It's similar to how I feel when a good friend comes to visit and I open the door to her cheery face. At first, before words even come, I feel something rich inside. The blessing of my friend. The gratitude I have for her presence in all the times that have come before - in all those times before I opened the door. Before we exchanged good-hearted hugs. Before the helpful, healing conversations that always came next.

So it is with our time spent with Spirit. When this true friend of ours is knocking on the door, and we open it, it's only natural to express our overwhelming gratitude! It's our own way of saying, "So glad to see you again!"

Today, as you open the door to Spirit, enjoy the next aspect of the Tea Ceremony by watching your teacup fill up with all God has given you recently.

Small Gratitudes, Good Hearts Make

In the few moments it takes to pour bubbling hot water in your teacup (or even when you heat it in the microwave), you have time to cherish a few small gratitudes. Two or three may seem too brief or too short a list, yet think how *this adds up if you do it daily during your teatime.*

Daily awareness of our many joys is certainly one good reason to let this small but substantive list form in our minds, but another reason is these sweet utterances simply make us happy. One of the biggest secrets is how sharing our gratitudes affects us. It's fun to see the exuberance of our daily gratitudes matched in the bubbling exuberance of our hot tea water, and to let our heart be glad. To let it be filled with gladness, for when a heart is filled with the bountiful goodness God provides, that heart is strengthened. And a good heart is ready to lead, to encourage - and to pray. *For isn't joy the kingpin of hope, and isn't the abundance of Love the strongest force in the Universe?*

Love Doesn't Stand Still

Even though we seek to stand still long enough to feel Love in our quiet teatime, when we start cherishing our gratitudes within even these small moments, we see that Love doesn't stand still! It's like that bubbling tea water. Exuberant! Flowing into places it can heal. Dancing with life. Energetic in its commitment.

What have you received that you are grateful for today? *If we look at the small and wondrous things within our day, instead of listing just the big general things, we find even more potently the miracles of Love's abundance.* Some people, when keeping journals, will say: "I'm grateful for my family." Wow, isn't that true! But if you look at this day's treasures, and say, "I'm grateful for the way one of my sons gave the other one a fish for his room today, and how it helped him through a time of loneliness. What a beautiful thing that was," - suddenly we're *noticing.* We're seeing the energy of Love working within our family - today - in the poignancy of these very tangible moments. And at the same time, we're seeing how the energy of Love changes things. Softens the corners of our days. And softens our own hearts along the way!

We all need this so much, too, for real life offers us tough challenges. I just got off the phone with my good friend, Judy, who had suddenly needed to dash her baby Isabella off to the hospital several days ago, as they faced a Meningitis scare. Truly, life is filled with plenty of things that can tax our spirit, but it struck me, as Judy and I talked about prayer, that acknowledging our blessings acts as a much-needed counterbalance to life's daily pressures. Even in times of stress, when we start our gratitude's list, however short, it starts changing our thought processes and naturally opens us to the positive kind of energy we need to bring to our prayer time. And once our hearts are filled with the memory of the joy and Love so inherent in these gratitudes, a newfound energy is released - an almost buoyant potential that transforms us first from within.

After Judy's phone call, my husband and I focused our prayers towards wonderful Isabella, but we started our prayer time differently. We started by celebrating the qualities we loved about her, and as we listed these easy-to-find things, our gratitudes, we stepped immediately into a higher level of loving energy. The happiness we felt about Isabella and about Judy and her family immediately began counterbalancing our fears in the situation. Yes, now we had opened the doors for prayer. It felt different, and it felt so good, as if some sort of change, some energy shift was already occurring, and the beauty of our happy hearts was a vital conduit!

So the energy of Love is not a "stand-still" kind of thing. Instead it contains the powerful energy of Light. We see it evidenced all around us. Just think about how a person's eyes are changed when they are filled with the spark of Love. They twinkle with a newfound energy - and that Light-filled energy changes us as we receive it! In my workshops, when we go 'round the table and take notice of our gratitudes - the people and things that are filling our lives with Love - I feel almost a golden glow take form within us. It's obvious how, as we become attuned to Love's presence, this small act of noticing changes our outlook. How our faces relax and sort of shine as we become a deeper part of that which we Love - as we hold more of that Love within our hearts. And more and more, we become filled with the energy of Light!

A Happy Heart Changes Things

My husband just called, and I felt that same kind of glow, but this time it was in his voice since I couldn't see his face. Not knowing what I was writing about, he proceeded to tell me how he was so grateful for things, like our new house - how it was a wonderful sanctuary of Light. (What a connection we have!) And he kept going, talking about the reasons he loved me. And how happy he had been just goofing around with our son this weekend. In such an easy way, he was proclaiming his gratitudes. Once again, I was amazed at how a happy heart changes things. How, in just moments, he had boosted my day with his delight in life and the blessings he found in it. Now the same good energy that he'd felt - and shared - was changing me!

Everyone I know has discovered a funny thing: that once you start doing daily gratitudes, you realize there are so many, you can't keep up with them. You can't count them all! And what a joy that is to our hearts, to know that abundance is a real thing. In truth, we can never count all the bubbles in our exuberant hot tea water, or all the water drops that make up a cascading waterfall, or all the joy that shines from a baby's eyes. Thank God for all things great and small - for by seeing just some of the small daily things, we realize how great the bounty is.

So it is, that when we take a moment while pouring our tea, and name a few of our blessings, our heart does a wonderful thing: it becomes resonant with Love's intentions. And something else happens: we realize this "preparation" time for prayer is an abundant time for us. It is not a time of waiting, but a time of rich and purposeful receiving. For as we name that which we love, we further receive it. It's as if we get to put our blessings in our shirt pocket and carry them around with us all day, all the while continuing to feel the joy of them! *The smile from someone who lights up your life. The kind gift from a son to his brother. The soft coos from baby Isabella.* This wealth of enjoyment is one of the beauties that comes from listing tangible real life blessings instead of vague generalities, for it enables us to hold these real life joys close to our hearts, where all good blessings go - and *they keep on blessing us.* I laugh as I think of it! Here we are, trying to thank God, and He is giving us yet another gift! He is continuing to gladden our hearts! And I figure, if He is so wondrously trying to expand our ability to receive, we'll just have to go along with it!

With this happy heart that comes from listing our blessings (however short or quick that list might be), we start reclaiming something more valuable than gold. *We begin reclaiming the desire to give again. To give back just some of the abundance we've been given.* I say some, for we know we can never gift back all that we've been given. And in response to this worthy desire, we begin to pray from a full and happy heart. Our energy generous and kind. Full of Love's expression, devotion, and a very personal delight.

Now prayer no longer feels like a heavy responsibility or a task-like obligation, one we don't have time for in our daily lives. Instead, as we watch the bubbles exuberantly dance into our teacup, we feel a deep and abiding opportunity - to give back just some of the abundance we've been given.

Accepting God's Bonuses

As we make a practice of noticing our blessings, often we start seeing something else that changes us deep inside: we notice that sometimes when we least expect it, God is bonusing us! Sometimes, it's hard to accept some wonderful things that come through our door. I know when we moved into this house, that I said, "God, this is so beautiful, I'm having a hard time accepting it."

And He said, "But don't you know I'm bonusing you?! I loved the way you listened to me, and stopped working to take care of your son when he had long-term medical needs. You and your husband both did your part to help, and even put off buying your house until now, like I wanted you to, so now I'm bonusing you."

I laughed as I accepted even more of God's Love! Yep, just when I think I can expand my heart and receive your daily blessings, you do this to me, I thought! And then as I talked to my husband today, we both realized God was bonusing him again. He had to miss work yesterday because of a power outage, so this morning he was getting double orders from unexpected customers. It's fun to realize when God is bonusing you (even when you haven't asked for it) - because then you can really enjoy it, and receive it!

Whether it's a blessing, either large or small, one

asked for or one coming as a complete surprise, when we bring a beautiful empty cup to the table and see the blessings God has already put into that cup, we start to see things differently. No wonder we smile in delight as the exuberant hot tea water bubbles into our cup. Prayer time had already begun! For God had already been answering ours. Most certainly, we think, our happy heart is ready to pray for those we love. In fact, by celebrating our gratitudes, maybe we, too, have already begun!

Part II:

The Art of
Receiving & Renewal

Letting Your Tea Steep

Merging with the Divine.

Most good things in life take time. Whether it's listening to a child, or letting our tea steep, over the years a wise person learns not to rush things, but to take the time that is needed. In our Tea Ceremony, we practice doing this, intentionally relearning the art that remembers the pace of Love. We stop rushing and adjust to Love's gentler gait because it immediately makes us feel better, but also because it's the beautiful power we want to harmonize with in our prayer time. We do have to make an effort though. Maybe we've left the hubbub of family and home; or gardens and chores; or jobs and schedules we'll soon return to, but we've all done one thing: we've chosen to take time. Ah-h, the beauty of time.

Simplicity Has Its Own Rewards

In itself, the beauty of time is such a powerful gift and can create such enormous changes. If we look back upon our lives, we'll most surely find almost all the good things we've accomplished, built, or experienced have: 1) not only taken time; but 2) most importantly, have been filled with a certain quality of time. The best moments of our lives and the best things we've accomplished have been filled with a craftsmanship we can all attain, one that's charged and directed by our own personal thunderbolt - one I would call *the here-and-now-beauty of our own attentiveness.* So easy to attain, so wonderfully within our reach.

I think about some of the best moments of my life, simple memories that please my heart to this day. I think about watching my boys play soccer - and laughing with them as we experienced the joy and freedom of those clean clear autumn days together. To this day, I feel the love that was in those sweet moments. I think about moments with my husband. Taking time to really hear him, see him, and be close to him. What else is necessary in moments like those? And I think about making a simple summer lunch. On a hot day, how good the fresh salad greens, the warm chicken, the surprise of red onions and mandarin oranges. The smiles on my family's faces as they dig in with gusto. All these things may be "small" things, but they feel very big in my memory. These are the things I'm thinking, as I pick up the string to my tea bag, and gently swirl it through the hot water. I can take time . . . and I can experience the blessings it brings me.

What is it about this process of finger touching tea bag, and tea bag touching water that instantly begins to center me? I really don't know at first. All I know is that it's just me and the tea. It's not me and endless telephone calls, or me and the mish-mash of the many projects in my day. No, now it's just me and the tea, and there seems something very right about that. Simplicity definitely has its own rewards. It reminds me of many priceless moments before - when all I did was take time to be aware of what life was wanting to offer me.

The Beautiful Process of Letting the Tea and the Water Blend

I love the something special that happens when synergy occurs, and one plus one equals three, so I watch with interest at what happens as the tea and hot water meet. How they are separate at first. But then as I drift the tea bag around the cup, how the essence of the tea and the warm receptivity of the water meet and merge. It's in these moments of letting our tea steep that we can see a parallel need in our personal spiritual lives. How important it is to take time to let God in, and let Him merge with our lives. If God is the tea and we're the water, we're changed into something more by the process, as we allow God into the mix of our lives.

When we pay attention to ourselves, our emotions, and what our real stresses and needs are in any here-and-now-moment, we start this process, for we become the cup of warm receptive water. But how often do we cover up who we are and what we need instead! At the end of a hectic day, we might have the tendency to just keep going, like the Ever Ready bunny, on some kind of automatic pilot we can't seem to turn off.

Even when we want to change this pattern, in the pressure of the moment, we may not remember how. At this point, the Tea Ceremony is such a friend to us, for in times of busy-ness or exhaustion, we can simply hold our teacup in our hands and watch the beauty of what happens as the tea and the water blend. Thankfully, God meets us where we are and how we are. And fortunately for us, that's how God likes it, for the process of healing can begin only when we bring our honesty, our translucence.

The surprise? When the waters of who we are meet the tea, we know we are not alone - and were not meant to live as if we were! We know instead, that there is much to receive, much Love and guidance that can warm the cup of our life. And to merge with the Divine is not such a difficult thing. In a Girl Friend's way, we know that we only need to add the tea, and take time to let it steep.

Centering, By Using Our Senses

Staying in the presence of the Divine is an awesome thing. Once we feel the natural kind of Love that wants to merge with us, and infuse our life with insights and wisdoms we can really use, we want to stay in that sacred place. Yet that place does have its mysteries. How was it that we got there? And how can we stay there?

We stay centered by the same route that we arrived - by taking the time for *mindful noticing.* Of course, first we set our purpose: we wanted to be with and merge with the helpfulness of Divine Spirit's presence, and feel that Lovingkindness completely within our spirit - instead of viewing this help as something extraneous, like a fixture we looked at from afar, unable to aid us in our daily lives and challenges. But after setting that intention, there are some creative secret steps that will aid our journey. The act of centering has long been practiced by many cultures. From monks, to artists, to musicians, to mothers in prayer for their children, centering is a key feature for opening our hearts to receive - but it longs to be understood better, so we can more actively use its creative power.

A monk uses it, for instance, when he lights a candle to pray. Today many people use the art of centering when they simply pay attention to the movement of their feet as they walk a labyrinth. An artist uses it when she concentrates on music to open her to the rhythm of creativity as she begins to paint. A musician uses it when he finds the emotional center of who he or she is amongst the images of life all around - and chooses the ones that fit. And a mother uses it when she imagines her child and feels how much she loves her son or daughter as she begins her prayer.

In the Tea Ceremony, the process is both fun and easy, for again it is a process of noticing. We might center ourselves by holding the cup, and by feeling its warmth infuse our fingertips. We might smell the fine aroma of the tea as it rises to meet us, and notice how our lungs expand, suddenly awake and ready for a new breath of life. Or we might take time to enjoy stirring the tea with a spoon, feeling its delicacy, watching the motion as the tea blends.

As we breathe it all in, the fragrance, the luxury of the moment, we most naturally glide into the here and now. In this place of simplicity, the fuss of life can fall away. The roar of the mind, the noise of life and all its expectancies. Instead, we stand in the here and now, and in such a beautiful way, it is enough. And we are enough.

Gently, we become one with the natural flow of life - and the gentle pace of Love. It is here, in this stillpoint, where the sacred resides. And it is our responsibility (to ourselves) to get there. To be there as often as we can - whether we are deeply in prayer or we are watching our boys play soccer, or we are washing dishes, or talking to a friend. Becoming mindfully present in the here and now allows us to deliciously slow down - to God's time. Where there is time for Love, time to appreciate, time to ask consciously, and time, especially, to receive.

There Is a Place,
the Stillpoint of Peace . . .

One of the greatest secrets is that there is a place where we receive. Not a geographic place, but this place of harmony: *the stillpoint of peace.* It's a warm and welcoming place, where our hearts feel so comfortable, we can set our burdens down, and be tended. It is in this place of harmony that we can most profoundly let Higher Spirit into the mix of our lives, and it's also the most powerful place we can pray for a friend, too. Rather than dashing off a worry-filled prayer that is really more worry than prayer, we may do things differently. We may take a few valuable moments to let our tea steep, to merge with the Divine, and harmonize with it as we mindfully pray for a friend. As we do so, we may realize more than ever how much we receive in the process, and find ourselves wanting to pray more, for our hearts are happy, *content beyond measure to be in the stillpoint of God's Love.*

A Sip of Warmth
That Spreads Through You

Receiving Comfort
- Body, Mind & Spirit Style.

A sip of tea, a sip of warmth. What a wonderful thing it is when we offer this simple thing to a friend, or a child who is ill, or a homeless person who comes in from the cold - for to give comfort is one of the kindest things we can do. And to take in a bit of comfort is also one of the kindest things we can do for ourselves. How amazing that it can begin with a simple, heartwarming sip of tea!

A Change in Perspective,
A Change in Heart

It's very hard to take a sip of warm and fragrant tea and not be changed a wee bit, even if we're *not* thinking at that moment about upping our spiritual game. But if we do change our perspective, and see this as a spiritual act, wow, how it opens up possibilities. And the biggest possibility is a change in the heart.

If we take a sip of warmth - Spirit's loving warmth - and feel it start to spread through us, we immediately begin to awaken our body-mind-spirit connection. And when we see the energy of that sip of warmth extend into the area of our heart, it makes the biggest difference, for the heart chakra is the center of higher Love's presence. When we are calm within our heart-center, everything can feel right within our world, for its peace radiates out like the center of the sun itself, and warms not only our own body, mind & spirit, but extends so naturally into the hearts of others as we let go of our limited ego-selves and enter into the loving world of prayer.

"This is some kind of healing!" you might say. And I would say, "Yes, 100 times yes!" This is the megawatt glow that can change our perspectives, change our intentions, and gently but very powerfully change our lives. It begins, quite gracefully, by accepting the kind of warmth that heals you, so you can then extend that expansive healing energy to others. But it must begin within us, within our bodies, so we let the warmth of God's Love change us from the inside, out, so we can then let it affect our mind (so we might direct our thoughts and therefore our intentions knowingly), and affect our spirit - so it might be one of joy and generosity.

What's My Body Got to Do With It?!

"But what's all this about my body?" you ask? Well, funniest thing, the last I checked, we were all living in one! So Spirit must have a reason, in fact probably a multitude of terrific reasons. But the best way to learn what this body-mind-connection stuff is trying to tell us is to think about your body. In fact, when was the last time you thought about your body?

Maybe it's seven o'clock at night, you've just collapsed into this big chair after work, dinner, dishes and who knows what else, and probably you're like most of the rest of us: the last thing on your mind is your body. In our society, we've almost taken this for granted. We expect to forget about our bodies. After all, production is the key. Getting things done. Well, in the process of "getting things done" we often kill the real richness and meaning of life. We push and pull at its rhythm until it obeys our demands for more, more, more. And our body is punished in the process. We not only forget to breathe, but we forget to relax our muscles or our mind, so regeneration can occur.

If we went to the store, we'd know it if we forgot our purse or wallet. If we got into our cars, we wouldn't expect it to start if we'd forgotten our keys. But do we acknowledge the basic needs of our bodies in the same way? Do we expect our mind and heart to give us good ideas and inspiration if we haven't had time to rest and recuperate?

If Your Body Is Saying Ouch, It Can Be a Good Thing!

"How does that work? How can my body saying 'ouch' be a good thing?" you demand! "It's the end of the day, I'm an absolute mess, and now you tell me that my body talking back to me is a good thing?!"

Well, yes it is. Your body is a spectacular network of signals designed with your spirit in mind. If we view each signal as a potential connection with Higher Spirit's desire to ease our pain, and heal us in every which way, then it all begins with listening to the signals we're being sent. In essence, God is talking to us through our body.

Spirit knows where we live, so Divine goodness comes right to us, no intermediary necessary. We have a direct connection! In this way, our body is so divine. If it squawks, or says it has an owie of any kind, it's providing a pathway of personal clues that can lead us into fresh insights and wisdoms - but first we are asked to relax!! To get in touch. To listen to a body that has been ignored, that smarts a bit from the lack of attention - attention it deserves, and needs in order to replenish our spirits, so we might create again in the happiness of prayer time.

Letting the Warmth of Love Move Through You

Oh, what a "job" it is to let the warmth of Love move through us! How simply awful it is to "have" to spend time doing this!! Thankfully, God loves us so much that He gives us easy ways to come back into harmony and alignment with the kind and healing power of Divine Love. I laugh happily a little now, as I simply take a sip, a soothing sip of warm tea, and let it enter my being in a sacred way.

Thank You, God. Thank You for loving me this way.

That you are right here, right now, in my everyday life in such an easy way.

And as I take a sip, I invite Love in. And I let its sunshine warmth move through me - into my heart-center, so I may feel Love's generous presence, and let it affect me, from the center of my being, out into each part of me.

As I let that warm and loving Light radiate through each part of my body, from my head to my toes, I let it touch all the tight places - and soften them. And relax them, so they might chat with me as they are filled with Love's healing ways. Even though I'm familiar with it now, it's still surprising to me that these tight places have something to say. There is usually a reason they are hurting, and the hurting goes beyond the physical. I've found that if I simply ask or pay attention, the area that hurts will give me a clue, either in a visual image, a symbol, or a feeling tone that carries a message.

I could see a stone, for instance, and see it become a flower - and understand I need to give my softer side some time to dream, and be with Spirit's flowering within me. Or I could see a knotted rope in some area of my body, and know it is a blockage. A place where emotions are tied up. "What is needed for healing here?" I might ask. And understand that forgiveness (giving things to God and letting go) will allow me to untie the knot, let go of the negative influence that maybe a person's actions had brought into my life, and live lighter. So then, in my prayer time, I might place that person in my hand (making the person's negative power smaller in the process!), and lift the person out and up to

God, and feel inspired to lovingly pray for that person to be filled with God's Love and Light instead.

As we let a sip of warmth spread through our bodies, we gain not only comfort, but some inner learnings, some real surprises - for we've set our limited egos aside, full of stressed-out, fear-based thinking - and we've allowed the sunshine of God's Love to guide us with a more expansive wisdom that contains healing in all kinds of ways.

Little did we know that so much wisdom could come into us - through honoring our body's connection with Spirit - and doing so in such an easy way! With a newfound grace, we let ourselves accept the Love that always awaits our simple but heartfelt request. This is a process that really offers up results, for when we accept Love in our quiet time, we find there is more Love to give. In this way, the body has its own kind of prayer, for as the body relaxes, so, too, does the mind, and the heart. And suddenly the world is a much kinder and gentler place, full of clues that seem placed by angels, so we might find them if only we look - or feel. With this kind of sustenance for the spirit, who said that gaining enlightenment couldn't be relaxing?! A veritable mystery - body/mind/and spirit style - that was *meant* for us to unfold . . .

There's a Reason a Teacup Has a Handle!

Getting a Grip on Strong Emotions.

Sometimes when we think of Prayer, we think it's an easy thing, and the hardest part is just finding time to do it. But as we really get to it, some days we find it *isn't* so easy - because as we expand our hearts to let God in, we come upon some stumbling blocks, some big ol' stumbling blocks right here - within ourselves.

These blocks are called by many names. Fear. Anger. Worry. But we know them well. Often when we want to move forward in our lives or help others do so, we lift up a prayer and unexpectedly encounter what we think must certainly be its opposite - some pretty hot emotions of doubt.

But to Divine Spirit, who loves every part of us, this is not the opposite of prayer, but a part of the inner translucent journey of prayer. A part of us that is crying for attention, and, from our Divine Creator's perspective, crying to be healed. Thank goodness, God doesn't judge us now, but celebrates our journey inward instead, and is ready to give us tips!

A Hand Up, a Handle on "Hot" Emotions

In the rush of strong emotions (such as: "Whoops, I really can't pray for this wonderful thing"; "It's impossible" - or – "I feel angry that this situation I want to pray about even happened"), it's hard to keep our balance, but thankfully God has not only great compassion, but is generous with His wisdom, for He gives us such obvious tips - even when we're having tea. After all, who hasn't had the experience of picking up a teacup, and then quickly setting it down again because it was too hot to handle?

In the Tea Ceremony, Spirit wants us to think of our emotions the same way. When our emotions are too hot to handle, set them down. Don't ignore their existence, but let them cool a bit. Within the handle and the teacup, there are many keys . . .

There Are MANY Reasons a Teacup Has a Handle!

Fortunately, a teacup offers us a handle, and in a spiritual way, it comes in useful during prayer time. Take, for instance, the traditional English teacup, made from a porcelain that reflects our own delicacy, but blessed with a handle that gives us an option: a way to hold something that could scald us, but hold it in a way that disperses the heat - or the pain!

That's the way Higher Spirit works in our prayer time. He gives us a handle, so we might hold onto our prayer until the hot emotions of fear or hurt or worry or doubt cool enough to be dealt with. And how are they dealt with? By letting God into any surprising negative emotion that arises. *If you're like most of us, often we haven't let Spirit into our doubt or our fear. Or we haven't handed God our honest hurt, frustration, or anger at a situation. But prayer time brings just this sort of thing up, and is meant to do so.* What part of our lives are we keeping in the shadows, that is ready to be healed? Maybe even yearning to be healed. The benefits to this time of sacred surrender are multifold, for even when we pray for someone else - our son or daughter or a close loved one - we often find we experience a healing of our own heart, mind and spirit in the process. I know I have! In fact, I'm rich territory for healing every day!

This handle for the teacup is meant to ease every-thing, and also to guide us. "Hold onto the handle (or God) if the cup's too hot." But a bigger gift comes with that. For now, each time we reach for the handle of our teacup, we can remember the kindest and most powerful thing of all - *that we are not alone.*

Matching the Mellow Warmth of Love

If the teacup's handle changes us and helps us deal with our fears and doubts by reminding us we are not alone, then the teacup's heat is the second tip Spirit gives us to improve the power of our prayer time. In its own beautiful fashion, the Japanese teacup demonstrates the importance of

noticing the heat, and therefore the tone of our own emotions, so we may seek to use our emotions for the good,
instead of having them use us.

As we put our hands around a teacup with no handle,
we even more directly feel its heat, and know, without being
told, that we need to let the tea cool to a mellow warmth
before we proceed. In terms of our emotions, when we let
them cool down a bit, we learn to match our emotions with
those of Higher Spirit. We can take time, in the middle of
prayer time fears and doubts, or even in the middle of an
argument, to ask ourselves - "What does Higher Spirit want
me to do with this?" "How can I match the tone of God's Love
right now?"

Instead of the flashes of hot emotions that threaten
our hopes and dreams, we can actually realign our emotions
to match those of Lovingkindness, of Higher Wisdom - and
feel this strong and now beautiful warm emotion within our
Heart Center. In a funny way, even negative emotions open
us to feeling the strength of emotions - and now the powerful emotion of Love - that is used to create. For prayer is an
act of creation. It is not an act of sitting beside the road, but
one of active involvement - and Partnership.

So we ask ourselves - what are we partnering with?
Our fears? Or that which we Love? So many times, we have
been unknowingly giving our energy and attention to the
negative - to that which we fear! By shedding the light on
our fears in prayer time, we are actively tackling that bad
habit, and changing the direction of our energies. We now
become conscious of our fears, our emotions - and make some

decisions. We decide to let God help. And we decide to learn what it is the Divine Universe holds as opportunities for us in these problems that now become our prayers.

We can instantly start learning a lot about matching God's loving tone as we hold a teacup in our hands. It will immediately signal us as to whether our emotions are too "hot" - and we need God's mellowing influence of Love before we continue - or whether we are ready to sip our tea, and be attuned to Love's full and life-changing presence during our prayer time. Only when our fingers can hold the teacup comfortably in our hands are we ready to proceed. And partner with the Divine.

The Bonus of Finding the Balancing Point

There are many bonuses to taking time to settle into the Tea Ceremony. As we face the emotions of fears and worries that seem bigger than life, we can hear God say, Softly and gently, set them down here, by the Love that waits to heal them. *Let your emotions still be honest and real, but let me into them, so you won't run your life by them - but by the guidance of my Love instead.*

In my own life, I think about what a relief it is to know I'm so thoroughly and magnificently cared for, and that God is there, like the handle of the teacup, in all things. Ready to provide the comfort, protection, and guidance I need to face my pain and fears, and let go. Let go into the mysterious healings and insights and luminous ideas that sweep through me in prayer time. What a great exchange it is. By releasing my fears and doubt, I've received so many things. A feeling of Love. A word for a friend. The rhythm of a child's recovery, and what to do, when. And so much more. Just think of your own life, and all you receive when you let Love fill the air!

As we open our Heart Center to Higher Guidance, we find a lifelong bonus: inside us, the Balancing Point. The sweet place of the soul, where we may rest and receive, and become a part of something More. As we hold our teacup, we feel the steady warmth of God's tenderness. The power of His healing presence. And the strength of His hope for us: in all things, in all ways, to turn toward Him in prayer - and in the beauty of this partnership, be forever changed. Inspired and expanded by the gentle force of Love.

Raising Your Teacup;
Raising Your Vibration

Attuning to a Higher Vision.

How often do we start our day without a vision? Or continue through our afternoon as if we're on automatic pilot - letting the business of life overtake the poetry of our soul, and the song it yearns to sing?

Most of us don't want to live a life of dull greys, devoid of Purpose, deprived of the beautiful song Purpose brings to our days. If we take a moment, we see ourselves living a life that feels much lighter - the scene in full color. Filled with a bit of play. A bit of love. And a bit of meaningful giving along the way. Just thinking about it puts a smile on our faces. So how do we recreate this rainbow-style of living, and stay in its welcoming energy?

Just Raise Your Cup!

This step in the Tea Ceremony is most assuredly one of my favorites, for it gives us such a nifty, easy-to-remember way to change the vibrations of our day. *Just lift your cup, and raise your vibrations to match that of the Divine*

Creator! This thought is so simple I could remember it in my sleep! And maybe that's the point. Maybe we're living life as if we're asleep when we're out of sync with Higher Spirit's energy - an energy filled with a radiant sunshine that wants to warm and lift all aspects of our life.

In this cool new Tea Ceremony, one of life's secrets to happiness is in our hands, for we are quite literally holding a teacup in them. The eternal question is always what we will do with it. As we raise that teacup to take a sip of refreshment, we can choose to consciously raise the vibration of our thoughts, so our prayers are filled with Love's awesome and life-giving creative energy. In such a nice way, the decision is in our hands.

At this point in our workshops, people start smiling a lot, for sometimes big Ah-Ha's are captured in small How-To's! "What a wonderful way to practice making a shift in my attitude, and aligning it with God's," people say, a bit ecstatic that they don't have to spend 3 hours of deep contemplation to "get it," for on some days 3 hours or 30 minutes seem hard to come by! Now we list our teacup on our gratitude's list, thankful for such a creative and easy-to-attain way to raise our spirits in the middle of our everyday lives. In fact, we lift our cups in gratitude, feeling a whole new kind of energy in this age-old salutation.

Reminding Ourselves We're Artists

Sometimes we forget an important fact - that God put a bit of an artist in each one of us. If you rebel at this idea, maybe it's because you've never been told *you are creative, and you were born to fulfill that creativity.* As a creativity coach, I've obviously taught many people from different walks of life about this, and have found that sometimes people don't think about their creativity, or they claim it's something they don't possess. But you don't have to be a painter or musician to be an artist. Instead God makes it so easy for us. All you have to do is want to put your loving energy into a seed of something that wants to grow.

In our prayer time, we have the opportunity to give our attention and our love to many things that want to grow. Maybe it's the love in one of our relationships. Or the health of someone we know. Or the direction of our work path. God smiles when we bring any of these things into the place where Spirit's loving guidance can infuse them, and bring sonorous comfort, healing, and wisdom into the equation. For the equation already exists, and stands empty, like a fallow field, waiting for the seeds to be planted and tended as we partner with God's sunshine in all things, big and small.

By bringing our hopes and dreams into prayer time, we activate this creative artist that God has put so wisely within our spirit. Indeed, God hopes for our dreams and our goodly desires. He hopes for us to be aware of them. And then to take time for them - and tend them in our Quiet Time of Prayer. He gives us a cup to lift for a reason, that we might recognize - and then honor - the creative spirit within us. So we might become filled with His awesome Sunshine as we lift ourselves into His true creative realm.

Optimism Isn't Out of Fashion; We're Just Out of Practice

What we find when we start raising our cup, and raising our vibrations, is that - shock of shocks, we've been living in some lower vibrations a lot of the time! These are evident when we see how often we've been imagining the worst instead of the best. In fact, we're quite good at imagining the worst. Our "intellect" might even be telling us that it's "the truth" - and it's more rational to just live with it, and not hope for more. Although acceptance of what we cannot change is a healthy life-skill and a healthy part of prayer at times, we need to actively challenge our own inertia, our own lazy way of thinking, and find out what part prayer can play in the situations we or our loved ones face.

Imagine instead the flower seeds my good friend Kathie gave me. A packet of colorful Cosmos so full of jubilance I can hardly wait to plant them! Should I treat them as we do some of our hopes and dreams, and think, "These won't grow anyway. Why should I plant them? It's only wishful thinking that they will grow"? No way, of course! We all know these seeds are meant to grow.

In this way, God is telling us that *some good thing is meant to come from each seed, or each prayer to which we give our energy.* It's not good enough just to have something to pray about - for that could still be classified as a "worry" or a "fear" - but our actions and our attitudes about it are the keys. The keys God waits for us to use. Just as the negative doubting-Thomas kind of intellect could stop us in our tracks, our attitude of optimistically lifting our attitude up into God's stratosphere can set us free. Free to remarkably co-create with Spirit. Free to find wisdom's path through confusing situations. And free to find God's tremendous power and comfort within all things. In prayer, we may not always get the bicycle we pray for, but maybe we are direct- ed to go walking instead - and bump into a friend that we help along the way. And suddenly, our life is filled with the Purpose that brings sunshine into our common days. But we would not find that Purpose, or that bright sunshine, with- out practicing a bit, and first lifting our hopes into God's welcoming arms.

Overcoming Inner Obstacles by Gentle Re-Attunement

Have you ever been in an aerobics class when the instructor asked everyone to "kick it up a bit - into a high- er level"? That's the same thing we do when we lift our teacup. We start raising the level of our thoughts, by kick- ing them up a notch! The first way to do that is to know which level we are working at now. In aerobics, we know when our body's engine is cold, and we need a warm up. In the Tea Ceremony, we've gone through our own form of warm- ing up, by setting our worries down. But now we want to really clear the cobwebs out, and enter into a high-energy workout.

In God's terms, that workout is still gentle, but it is a re-attunement, for His sphere is full of possibilities and thunderous insights, and guidance that can change your life, one prayer-filled step at a time. In my meditations for women, "Walking With the Flowers," I mention how we can re-attune ourselves and understand God's creative energy by looking at flowers. I was especially affected by looking up at an arbor of outrageous Sweet Peas as they unfurled their vibrant color against a china-blue sky in the Butchart Gardens near Victoria, British Columbia. It was one of the first times I really thought of God's energy as a vibration. The vision of it left me humbled at its radiance, and at the same time, *it made me want to match that energy whenever I could.* Maybe in some way, this was the point of life itself. In all things, to attempt to match that Higher Thought Vibration, and all the potential it can bring into being.

For this reason, it's valuable to think about the energy within things – and, more specifically, *the energy we put into things!* If, as it's said for instance, the cells of our body change every given number of years, and those cells are composed of vibrating energy, then we may start thinking of the energy that flows within everything, and realize it can be changed. How it is affected by our thinking. By our attitudes that we find deep within our hearts. It's important then, in daily life and especially in prayer time, to ask ourselves if our attitudes are ones of healing, and ones of opening to possibilities? Or are they ones of defeat - even as we *think* we're praying?

One way to test this is to see what vision comes to us as we pray. What picture presents itself? Pretend you have two TV sets at the moment. One is black and white, and one is color. Imagine the challenge, problem, or concern you bring to God in prayer at first on the black and white TV set. Let yourself see the problem or issue in its negative form. Then turn to the other set, and see the possibilities in full and vibrant color. See a loving expression of your hopes and dreams in beautiful fulfillment - and see all you've learned along the way.

Now go back to how you were thinking about your concerns as you started giving them over to prayer. Did you have the black and white set on? Or were you seeing it in full color - in the Higher Vibration of possibilities that want to come into being? If it's black and white, you might want to practice your spiritual aerobics, lift your teacup, and kick up your thoughts into a higher vibration. Then let yourself stand in the energy of that Love! It's one of the best forms of gentle re-attunement we can practice, for *it helps us see - and then decide - if we want to live our life by default, or by Purpose and creative vision.* If we want to live our live in the dull colors of black and white, or in the wider spectrum of vibrant colors the Sweet Peas know about.

The Rainbow Energy of Higher Spirit's Light

When we lift our thoughts and enter into the energy of Higher Spirit's Love, it's exhilarating. It's a rainbow kind of energy that can change us from the inside, out! As we lift our cup and learn to align ourselves with this Divine Energy, we feel more like a harp, its strings finely tuned, ready to play the songs that come from the heart of God.

As this energy fills us, sweeping through our body until we feel resonate with Love's higher intentions, *we stand upon the Rainbow Bridge, and let the expansive Light of Love, Compassion, and Healing change our life.* It is here our Prayers and their Answers merge. It is a place of Angels and Butterflies, insights and winged flight. It is a place both humbling, and of such sacred personal power that we begin to lead differently. Creating not by demand, but by opening our hearts to Love's Vision - then helping it grow, like a flower, into its full expression in our life. And then encouraging that song of Purpose, day by beautiful day.

Do we still want to start our day without a vision? Or walk through it on automatic pilot, tossed to and fro by the wind? No thanks! We'd rather use this Girl Friend's kind of tool, and lovingly practice a bit - to lift our cup, and lift our vibrations into a place that creates a Rainbow Bridge of Love, and a Light that beams forth from our heart each day.

Enjoying High Tea - A Serving of Rich Blessings

Honoring Abundance - by Using It in Your Life.

Imagine experiencing High Tea in a traditional English house surrounded by lush rose gardens - all on the grounds of the world famous Butchart Gardens just outside of Victoria, British Columbia - what a yummy thought to most busy people! From cucumber sandwiches, to chocolate trifles, to the aroma of Earl Grey tea or the most delicate Jasmine - ah-h, how good it feels to be served in this luxurious fashion. What has now come to be called High Tea is definitely a one-of-a-kind event for the spirit and for the senses, reminding us how great it is just to receive. But this act of receiving is one that Higher Spirit wants us to receive daily, not just occasionally. The blessings from "prayer time High Tea" come to us with the same delight, with a wonderful array of Ah-Ha Moments served to us on a beautiful silver tray, meant to bless our lives if only we take time to receive them.

The Art of Receiving . . .

"Is there such an art? If so, I want to sign up!" That's what most of my girl friends say, because it sounds to them like a bit of heaven! But fortunately, because of our own Tea Ceremony, it's a bit of heaven we've been getting accustomed to receiving - for we've been practicing.

Each time we relax, lift our teacups, and (as in the last chapter) attune ourselves to the Rainbow Bridge of God's higher vibration, we feel the difference as Love sweeps in with all its bounty of blessings. Rich blessings that satisfy us so much we think we must be eating chocolate! Indeed, a High Tea for our spirit. In this step of our Tea Ceremony you could actually eat a snack, but it's not at all necessary. Sometimes imagining the High Tea of blessings that come your way is more satisfying.

This art of receiving the High Tea of abundant blessings and answers to prayer may not come all at once though. It does take practice and we may feel it in slow increments, as we open our hearts enough to receive that which is so finely offered. The best of us will often find we've forgotten how to receive, as in the midst of our busy lives we forget to take time to accept the luxury of High Tea with Spirit. Or we may indeed get started, taking the first positive steps of prayer time, but stop before we receive the inspiration that awaits us. We may find ourselves acting much like the person at a banquet - who goes but who doesn't partake. The choice is ours. And the choice, incredibly, is how much we'll receive. Will we lead a life of spiritual poverty, or one of prosperous, life-changing abundance?

Deserving High Tea –
Using Our Spiritual Self-Esteem

Just as we might sadly deny ourselves the enjoyment of High Tea in a beautiful English Tea House, there are reasons we might deny ourselves High Tea with Spirit. It's imperative that we ask ourselves why we *wouldn't* let ourselves receive the relief that comes from talking with God - and handing over our problems, large and small. To answer that, it helps to think of one of your best friends for a moment. Is he or she deserving of an inspired word, a compliment, a kindness, or a helping hand? Would you deny her that? I don't think so, but we often deny it to ourselves. We still need our moments when we accept the High Tea of blessings and kindnesses from Higher Spirit. And, just as our best friend does, we deserve it.

We deserve it because we are one of a kind, and precious in the eyes of Spirit. *There is nobody else than you to do the giving that was meant to be done through you.* And to do that giving, each of us must take time to receive, so our soul may grow into it. Into the beauty of serving - by being served by Spirit. If we don't think we deserve this, our special time with Spirit, we are practicing low spiritual self-esteem. We're excluding God from the equation of our lives, and the very essence of who we are.

How do we practice high spiritual self-esteem? By knowing, deep in our heart of hearts, that we were born to receive. That the tray of rich Ah-Ha inspirations has our name on it. And the name of each of our best friends!

In God's eyes, we're a bloom ready to expand in the glory of His giving. To receive these many blessings, we first need to listen.

Practicing the Joy of Listening

Oh, what a joy it is to listen sometimes, instead of always do the talking! At times we forget that communication goes both ways. That's why, when we go to the prayer closet in a sacred way, and *listen* as well, it becomes a form of *communion.*

In this step of the Tea Ceremony, we get to do the most joyful thing - we get to Listen to the still place within us, where Higher Spirit resides. As we take our moments to surrender the problems or needs of our day, we lift our cup of tea and step into a higher vibration, participating in the High Tea with Spirit we'd yearned for all along. It's not enough to hear our own voice constantly. Instead, it feels so much better to have a two-way conversation, and Listen to our Best Friend. What a relief it is, for when we stand upon this radiant Rainbow Bridge of Love, we start finding the wealth that waits for us there.

But Listening is an Art. Most of us are not very good at pushing the pause button, to consciously create the sacred pause, where we can hear, feel, or come to know Higher Spirit's heartbeat - and the power of the Love that will work such blessings within our days.

So how can we Listen better? First of all, by knowingly deciding to do so. Just tell yourself, *"Now, I'm going to Listen. I'm going to open my heart and hear the answers and insights God has waiting for me. I'm going to open the door, and Listen to what Higher Spirit wants to teach me and give me today."*

In order to do that, to Listen with grace, it requires something of us that is also all too rare: we need to be humble. We need to stop honoring our problems, and putting them in the driver's seat so much that we don't give God a chance to answer them - with ideas that can break the log jams in our lives; add mercy and compassion to our days; and rev us up with new ideas.

It's good to ask ourselves when the last time was that we were humble. When was the last time that we let up on the accelerator and let God do the driving for awhile? Or that we simply asked God what He thought was important that we do this day?

It may sound so simple, but one of the best things we can do is simply ask ourselves if we're Listening - and then give ourselves time to do so. In the Tea Ceremony, these times can still be short and sweet, but because we're practicing by doing it more often during our tea breaks, we're building a habit God loves - for He can come to us more often. He's been invited in, and been invited back - and He's even found someone who wants to share time with Him, not only by talking but by Listening, too. And that must make God smile!

Tips to Improve Sacred Listening

Since listening in a sacred way is not our strong suit, we definitely can use some fun ways to strengthen that new skill. Here are a few to choose from. You might try them all, but use what works with you, and your lifestyle.

1. *Write It Down Sometimes.* (I say "sometimes" because this is an easy Tea Ceremony, and if it gets too complicated, it might not work for you, so use your own judgment. You may jot down notes on some days, but not on others, for instance.) After you've opened up your two-way communication, capture the insights you receive when you stand upon that radiant Rainbow Bridge. Even the greatest thoughts can be lost as the day cascades before you, so choose your own manner to write them down. Whether it's in a spirit journal in your favorite color, or on a post-a-note, write it down in a way you'll use it. By writing it down, you'll remember it longer, and be able to track your progress with your prayer time insights during the week.

2. *Put Your Insights in a Place You'll Stumble Upon Them All Week Long.* After you write it down (it can even be just a few short notes), don't lock it away in some corner you won't see all week. Open your journal or put some post-a-notes in your car or on the fridge. We all need refreshers if we're going to really understand the full import of the insights we've received. God's ideas are always big ones, even when they're about little things.

One of the many things God has taught me through His blessings of High Tea, for instance, is just to touch people softly - whether in word, or deed, or actual touch. That may seem like a "little" idea, but I've been living with it for years now, and every day I think about it, I am changed for the better. I have lots of room to grow, and God must know that, for He's there for me, helping me learn - but gladder still when I take the initiative, and honor His insights by putting them in a place I'll stumble upon, and practice using them in my everyday life.

3. *Choose a Learning Word for the Week - or Day.* Sometimes in Quiet Time, God will give us information that clusters around an idea. What if today's word was Mercy? How would it affect our lives if we decided to practice that for a whole week? Odds are, we would definitely learn more about it. And that wouldn't be a bad thing!

4. *Share It.* There's something beautiful that happens when we give voice to what we're learning. By speaking about it, we give it the breath of life. We let it expand into the atmosphere of our daily living. Plus we often find out insights our friends may be gaining about the same thing. Some of my best memories have been sharing insights about what we're learning from Higher Spirit with my husband, as we walk the road of discovery together, and let the aire crackle with good ideas.

5. *Feel the Affect It Has on Your Life.* Another easy way to multiply your listening power is to understand the impact God's good ideas are having on your life. In this way, we come to value them. And what we value, we repeat. Listening is suddenly one of our highest priorities because the good ideas that come from it are practical, and in a

thousand different ways, make our life better.

I think, for instance, about the gentleness of touch that I mentioned learning about in prayer time, and how it quickly and exquisitely makes my life better. It builds bridges of tenderness between my husband and myself; it helps me settle down and hear people better; and it helps me understand and honor my own healthy delicate nature - so I can give a bit of poetry to others, and to myself. Yep, I love these Ah-Ha's, and the way they make life better. Which brings me to the next important concept . . .

Realizing You Can Ask about Anything!

In prayer time, it is definitely High Tea. A rich array of blessings stand waiting for you. Most of all, they stand waiting for your awareness. Maybe we've thought to ask Higher Spirit to help with one thing in our week, but we haven't thought much further than that. But that's why we're taking this step in the Tea Ceremony, for when we start to Listen, we start to realize *how much God wants to give us, and help us with. It's hard to get our thoughts around this abundance - but it's our task to do so!*

What haven't you asked Higher Spirit to help you with this week? This question alone can change your consciousness - and change your life! Here's a fun way to start opening to the many blessings God wants to bring your way. Imagine the High Tea at the Butchart Gardens that I referred to in the beginning of this chapter. There are a variety of delicious things on the silver tray that's brought to your table:

- When you think about the *cucumber sandwich,* for instance, ask in what kind of *common way* does God want to affect your life this week. One everyday inspiration I received recently was to think of cleaning and beautifying one room at a time each day, instead of trying to clean and improve the whole house at once. That decreased my stress and brought an element of fun into the way I could creatively cherish each room. *How can you open up your everyday life to a bit of fresh inspiration?*

- When you think about the *chocolate trifle,* ask in what way God wants to bring you *a bit of dessert?* Ah, this is a fun question - and one we don't always ask! This week, the answer to that question came in the form of what Higher Spirit inspired me to give my husband for his birthday. One item was a chiminea for our back deck. When I first began looking for it, I couldn't even pronounce it! But this weekend, we built our first fire, and sat around it - our youngest son, my husband, and myself. We stopped all our projects and totally received as we gazed into the ever-changing flames that warmed us while we looked up into the brilliance of the starry sky. A starry sky I would have missed if I hadn't Listened to God's kind inspiration. A time of 'round-the-bonfire sharing I would have missed if I hadn't accepted *a bit of dessert* when it was offered.

High Tea of the Spirit? It's reflected in all the delicacies we're offered on the silver tray at a traditional High Tea, but the High Tea of the Spirit goes so much further. Straight into the heart of our lives, where Receiving is the cornerstone - to knowing God in all His forms. From meeting our most common needs to giving us divine desserts, God's serving of rich blessings brings a whole new spirit of prosperity to our lives. So much so, we may never again look at a silver tray without thinking of ALL God wants to give us, if only we let Him.

The Clink of Fine China

Using a Delicate Sound to Stay Centered & Aware.

If there were "little people" in Ireland and they could talk, the wee ones would probably say this step in the Tea Ceremony is a "wee one", but a fine one at that! For what better way to remind us to "stay tuned" during our prayer time, than to use the bell-like chime of fine china, as it clinks so artfully when we place our teacup on a beautifully decorated saucer? What better way to pull ourselves back into focus during our meditation time?

Calling Us Back from the Drift of Distractions

"Whew, I didn't know I was drifting!" That's what I and so many other people say when they realize they were drifting during their prayer time - drifting far away from the insights they may have already been receiving. Their mind suddenly lost amidst a world of distractions.

"How does this happen?" we all wonder. We had the best of intentions. But alas, one thought does lead to another, and our worries, problems, and even our best goals and dreams have lots of tangents they can take us on. So it's no surprise that the process of prayerful meditation brings up one of the biggest challenges: how to stay focused instead of getting lost in distractions!

Discovering this is a problem for everyone, not just for ourselves, is a big relief for the women and men in my workshops. As we look at each other and laugh at our all-too-easy ability to drift, we're actually gaining power - for a problem known can be a problem tackled. When we laugh at ourselves instead of beating ourselves up, we can practice lighthearted acceptance - and stay positive as we re-direct our attention. We can say "Yes, that's happening, but now I don't have to stay distracted."

Whew, that sounds good to me, for life is full of distractions, and saying we won't feel them in prayer time is practically setting ourselves up for failure. One of the best things about our Tea Ceremony is: *we don't have to be perfect.* So now, if we know those pesky distractions will pop up at times, we can have a plan, and *what is more fun and easy than to use the sound of our teacup to call us back into focus?!*

In NLP (neuro-linguistic programming) terms as I understand them, this is a method that can be used to change a habit successfully - by choosing something that reminds us of the new habit we want to practice. For instance, if a person wants to stop smoking, they may choose to put a rubber band on their wrist, and snap it when they feel the urge to smoke but want to choose their new behavior. In the same way, the clink of our fine china teacup can gently but very effectively call us back into focus, and is a lot more fun than the twang of a rubber band!

The Mindfulness in a Teacup

What a wee beauty this is, this fine china cup that can bring us back into alignment with Higher Spirit so easily! In each step of the Tea Ceremony, we've learned to listen in some way, *but now we're reminded to listen to ourselves.* Are we centered and aware? A modest teacup can help us do that, as each time we so naturally set it down, we hear the clink of china, and check in to see if we're drifting or "in tune."

This action, of setting the teacup down, and listening to ourselves while we do, reflects the process of prayer itself. It is not a passive thing, but an action. An action that truly becomes sacred when it is imbued with our intent. And our intent is manifest by our mindfulness. What a lovely way to stay in that zone of mindfulness than to mindfully set our teacup down, and listen to the sound our favorite teacup makes to call us home.

Returning Our Attention to the Delicate Power of Prayer

One of the reasons the sound of the teacup and the way it clinks so beautifully works for me, is it reflects the delicate power we find in prayer. As we've discussed before, we need to come to God in a loving and delicate way. We need to bring our real, heartfelt problems, and our deepest wishes and dreams to Him in prayer.

But as we offer Him our honest delicacy, we soon move to a higher zone. In prayer time, our delicacy is lifted up, and meets with the tenderness of God's heart. He offers us His delicacy - the powerful delicacy to understand us, to walk with our deepest feelings and yearnings, and to show us the mercy of His magnificent, unconditional Love.

As I set my teacup down, and hear the delicate clink of fine china, I'm often reminded of this - that God meets my delicacy with His own, and now my delicacy no longer has to be a distraction, but can be used for healing and renewed growth in a multitiude of ways.

In a most graceful fashion, this eases my transition, and gets me back on track. With a teacup in hand, and God at my side, I'm given new thoughts and inspirations that make me continually celebrate the delicate power of prayer.

The Clink of the Here and Now

Another reason the clink of our teacups works so well, is that a sound can call us back into the here and now. This is of great benefit, for when we're lost in distractions, we're not fully in the present. And *it is in the present that we can fully feel God's presence.*

That's why we can be healed during prayer time, for it is in the here and now that God can take any past experience, and fill it instead with the healing power of His Love. Then, we so kindly have a choice, do we want to keep the pain of the past, or let our life be filled with the power of His presence? In this sacred place of the here and now, we can let God in, and let go of memories that don't serve us well, for we're letting them be changed by the force of God's transforming Love.

Feeling the Spiritual "Bell-Tone" Within Us

Listening to the clink of fine china, and using it to remind us to come home, back into alignment with the fine energies of healing that God is giving to us, has a great pay-off, for it also helps us come to recognize that Spiritual Bell-Tone within us. When we feel "right with God," we feel right inside. Peaceful. Centered. Lovingly aware. And it is at this place that we most fully receive Higher Spirit's awesome guidance.

Knowing how this place feels helps us in our daily life. It helps us center ourselves instantly when we're in a group of people, or when we're driving (boy, can that be helpful!), or when we're disciplining our children, or when we're creating a new piece of art. Many books have been written on just such a thing - how to get to the place where you can be truly creative. How to get into the Zone. How to live in a feeling of Peace.

Our teacup may be a wee thing, but the sacred practice it brings us to is a great thing. Finding our Spiritual Bell-Tone is a treasure beyond measure, one that is personal, jubilant, and resonant - resonant with God's real gift, the here and now presence of His remarkable Love.

Part III:

The Art of Activating Love's Intentions

Sip-by-Sip, Step-by-Step Miracles

Sacred Co-Creating.

Isn't it fun to watch our children grow? Or see a tree leaf out and bloom in the spring? Little by little, step-by-beautiful step, amazing things happen. In prayer time it's helpful to bring that same attitude of patient wonderment, so we can watch miracles unfold - step-by-step, or as we would describe it in the Tea Ceremony, *sip-by-sip!*

What Would Happen If We Skipped a Step?

That's a great question to ask, and can be applied to many things. What would happen if we decided to skip a step in our child's development, for instance, and not be concerned about our child's desire to crawl? There are a few rare babies who skip this step, but most children benefit by crawling first, and developing the underlying strengths it takes to walk. Maybe it's building muscles. Or building up their balance. Or just learning they can really do things. But all of it is valuable - and the same thing applies to our prayers.

Each step in the process may be giving us something of great value. What if, within our own prayer steps, we built up our spiritual muscles? Or found our spiritual balance? Or "just" learned we can really do things? If we look at it this way, maybe skipping steps is not as glorious or beneficial as we first think – especially as it applies to wanting things sooner rather than later.

Sometimes we may be praying for our health, for instance, and of course want it instantly, but we receive the first step - an inspiration to stop eating or drinking something that may harm us and deplete our system. But what happens if we ignore this step? After all, it's not the complete and awesome miracle we were praying for!

When we try to fast-forward and look only for the splashy miracles, we often skip the very essentials God wants us to learn. If instead, we saw each answer to prayer as the special gift it was, we might encourage the full miracle that's trying to take place - and see what we're learning as maybe the greatest gift God is offering us. *For to learn to listen to God's tips as they come in - what a powerful skill that is!* Such a valuable personal skill, that once we think about it, we know it shouldn't be skipped at any price!

If we're skipping steps, we're like jet setters who want it all now. And somehow, that doesn't feel very peaceful or loving. As we skip all those steps in between, we may miss wisdom; practical information; and the honing of our spirit as it learns along the way. But we also miss something else: we miss opportunities for more of God's Lovingkindness, for if we're skipping steps, we're also skipping our time with

Higher Spirit. And as we receive God's Lovingkindness consistently over time, we change - growing both softer and stronger at the same time.

A Gentler Way: Step-by-Step

As we decide to ask God to be our partner, and let Him guide us over time, we open up to some mighty fine possibilities. We not only get to know Higher Spirit better (after all, it is a relationship!), but we also open up to God's design, and how we are a part of that design. Subtly, step-by-step, our spiritual intuition is strengthened, and we begin to see what we should do next. Instead of forcing the process, we begin to co-create with God, sharing input with our Creator, just as He asks us to actively participate, too.

As we go about things in this gentler way, we may adjust what we do, or how we do it. Before we give in to the impulse to push through things, we may check in with our Source and see if it's a good idea - or if the timing is right. At different times people have asked me to do something, and that something is even a good thing, but I've checked in, and knew the timing was not right. Instead, I waited, and miraculously, the situation was solved without any action or intervention on my part. But how do we know when is the right time to do something, and when isn't the right time? We don't - not unless we go with God in this gentler fashion, letting Him guide our steps, and the timing of them, for our best benefit.

Acknowledging Small Miracles, and Big Ones

In a previous chapter we talked about listing the insights we gained in prayer time as a way of improving our ability to sacredly Listen. A similar practice can help us find the pathway to big miracles - by noticing the small ones.

As I look back, I've received many miracles. Extraordinary ones! But somewhere along the way, I started noticing all the small miracles that took place before the big one popped into place. A big miracle can happen instantly, of course, but if we want to live a life of miracles, it's great to get in the habit of inviting them in. And God really enjoys a student who is ready to learn - because as we learn, we grow closer to God.

When, for instance, I healed from Rheumatoid Arthritis (which wasn't deemed possible by my doctor), I had a healing dream. During the healing dream, three healers asked me to meditate daily, and afterward, I did just that - most days. Even though I'm not perfect (and Spirit doesn't expect us to be), I definitely upped my spiritual time with God. In the process, I "stumbled" upon new ways to meditate. Soon I was doing my part (taking my steps), and letting God's loving energy in to rejuvenate my body, mind and spirit on much deeper levels - which affects me to this day, for it's one of the best gifts I've ever received.

But as it refreshed my mind, a new thought jumped in, and soon I acted upon that guidance. I added another healing step and stopped using a certain artificial sweetener. This was not the *only* part of my healing, but it probably seemed bigger to people looking in from the outside, for soon after, I was completely healed. Blood tests were suddenly normal. Pain and inflammation left my body. And I began dancing again. But most of all, I loved dancing with Spirit - step-by-beautiful step!

What would happen if we started more actively noticing the intuitive insights we're receiving? How would we feel if we paid attention to the steps toward our miracles, instead of just waiting for the big one? How would it change our lives, and the way we did things?

For me, it made prayer time even more fun, for I was constantly getting answers. Sometimes small things. Sometimes big bombshells of positive ideas that changed my way of thinking. And sometimes I came to the culmination of a prayer project, and just cried with happiness, opening my arms wide to accept the grace of it all.

The Power of Celebration

The Tea Ceremony makes paying attention to these step-by-step miracles even more fun, because now I can do it - sip-by-sip! This morning as I enjoy my Vanilla Nut Tea, I can feel that sacred step-by-prayer-step process reflected in the beautifully repetitive action of sipping my tea. But when we add the joy of celebration during this sip-by-sip process, we increase the power of our prayer-walk tenfold! For our joy - in each small miracle brought to us in each step - magnetizes us for more.

It's as if the energy is actively drawn to and once again, magnetized by our joy, our celebration. When we not only Receive miracles, but Appreciate them, the Divine Universe comes into some kind of spiritual alignment that radiates great creative energy. What we notice does increase, and in this wonderful process of following our joy, the happiness within us also increases. No wonder noticing what God does for us is one of the most joyous acts we can perform!

When we take this added step, and celebrate our step-by-step Journey with our Creator, God must create some new rainbows somewhere – just to show His happiness with us! Sip-by-sip, we can take time to remember, and celebrate all the lovely things we're receiving and learning on this Journey of faith. And by doing so, with each beautiful sip, we're gently increasing our faith. Step-by-step, sip-by-sip, we're finding a whole new way to let the power of Increase flow throughout the walk - and the dance - of our lives.

Even on the Shelf, the Teacup Talks

Finding Lovely Reminders.

It's fun to think back about the beginning of this book, and what motivated me to write it. I definitely wrote it for myself, because I wanted a way to remember - more often - to pray for a friend. What I received, much to my delight, was this fun Tea Ceremony. And one of the reasons it's fun is how wonderfully easy it is to do all, or even a part of it. At each step of the way, Spirit asked me to keep it easy - and I've got a grin on my face, because if you thought any of the other chapters was easy, this must be the easiest. But, ah-h, we all deserve a little fun, and isn't it great that God wants to share His JOY in the process of prayer with us?!

Now, he wants to help us *keep the vision and power of prayer going* - in such a delightful way . . .

Such a Beautiful Reminder!

Now that we've experienced a veritable bounty of loving prayer times during the many special days and more relaxed evenings with our Tea Ceremony, we have probably grown fond of our teacup - or perhaps many of them! So it's no surprise to us, that even on the shelf, the teacup talks to us. At this point, in our hearts and minds, the teacup is so much more than an ornament. Instead, it has become a beautiful reminder of our time with Spirit, and all we've gained there.

The best thing, of course, is that now, just by walking by and glancing at one of our teacups, it can remind us to pray. To send another loving thought up into the heavens of our day. What a simple way to easily keep in touch with the prayers we've already expressed for friends, beloved family members, or ourselves. Someone I love has a low white cell count, a depressed immune system. That can be depressing. But it changes things when I lift up this concern in prayer, and it changes my spirit and my day even more when I pass by my teacup, and remember that prayer again. For that prayer contains Love - and how Love changes things!

The Shape and Delicacy of Love

Even the shape of the teacup makes me feel so good, as I feel its ability to hold our concerns - Spirit's vast ability to hold our concerns within the chalice-like hands of God's Love. As I walk by, I can reiterate my prayer, but also let go, knowing my prayer is in good hands!

As God holds our concerns, I'm again amazed at how they are held with such delicacy, and I love the way the china reflects this delicately. As I've said before, at what other times can we be so vulnerable, as when we come to God in prayer? But now, just looking at the ivory bone china cup on the shelf reminds me how the Tea Ceremony so graciously teaches us to gladly bring this vulnerability to Higher Spirit, instead of fearfully locking our feelings away and letting them gain negative strength when repressed.

As I walk past my teacup, its delicacy has become a gift I treasure even more. Yes, it is OK to bring our worries here. It is OK to admit our weakness and our fears. It is more than OK to be human. For as soon as we express our concerns in a prayerful way, we ask for help, and we let our delicacy become a strength. As my teacup sits there, I know it's been so happy to be used, for now the shape and delicacy of Love are part of the very fabric of my day, offering me a chalice of comfort and strength that says I am never alone. Instead, I am cared for in this incredibly beautiful way!

The Flowers of Inspiration

This morning I looked at my new flower planters on the deck, and felt better immediately. Oh, the power of flowers to lift the heart and mind! And then I looked at my teacups. Almost all of them have flowers on them! In the same way that flowers lift our day, my teacup does so also. Just the beauty of them inspires me as I walk by, and now the act of seeing them on my teacup inspires me more, because it reminds me of all the real life insights that have bloomed within my prayer time.

If I've been praying for my mom, I can look at that

beautiful teacup, and feel the flower-like inspirations I received in prayer time - and send that same Love forth to my mom again. In the process, I'm doing what we could call "spiritual isometrics." As I raise myself into those higher vibrations, I'm using my spiritual muscles again - doing "reps"!! - and strengthening these valuable muscles, just by "tuning in" to my prayers as I glance at my beautiful teacups!

Colors That Call to Us

We know from past teatime experience, there's something about just choosing our teacups that is exquisitely satisfying. It is so personal that each time we choose the cup reflective of who we are and how we're feeling, we feel the *personal* Love God has for us. That day. That moment. So when I walk past my cup, I love the colors - of the cup, of myself, and of the prayers I now share with Spirit.

Some days, I notice the soft pink in the small roses on the cup Julie gave me. Ah, she knows me well - just as God does. And when I remember sipping tea from that cup, I recall sharing my fears with God about a new project on which I was working - then receiving the strong wings of Divine Spirit's guidance because of those prayers. Now that cup means so much more to me, because it reminds me how God reverberates within my projects and dreams, helping tender new ideas grow strong in the garden God wants my life to be. A beautiful reminder, these soft pink roses!

I also love my glorious red teacup embellished with

gold, for as I glance at it, I remember, in prayer time, how valuable God thinks we are. How we are this same kind of treasured cup to Him. And as I look at it, I want to serve Him well, with all of the Love and Beauty He puts into us.

There are many favorite cups of course, but lately I've fallen in love with a deep purple coffee cup. It's so much fun that I purchased extras and gave them to special friends. Even found excuses to do so! Knowing that all of us are sharing the same deep purple cup, one that inspires me just by looking at it, brings a whole new level of satisfaction and excitement when I see it. I think of all of us experiencing the art of Prayer and Tea and Thee, and my Girl Friend's heart is happy as I instantly send them my prayers, and appreciate the circle of Love we share.

Color can be used in some fun ways. As a group, you can all choose a cup with the same color and enjoy the unity and connected feeling using it inspires, or you can notice what cups help you pray for different people. Right now, for instance, I'm using a soft butter-yellow cup to pray for my loved one's white cell count to rise. Each time I see the warm glow of this cup, I think of a healthy immune system. The butter-yellow color seems perfect for this prayer request, and now, even if I'm not actually looking at the yellow cup on the shelf, I can see the cup in my mind - and let it lovingly align my heart with the healing power of God's radiant and oh so helpful higher energy.

The Teacup's Handy Handle

Not until receiving the Tea Ceremony had I appreciated how handy a teacup's handle is! As I glance at it, I'm so utterly grateful that God has provided a handle for our hot emotions. What a cool thing for Him to do! I look at a hot handle now, not with a feeling of heavy emotions, but with a new sense of peace that only comes from being sustained - in all times - by a Love so great, it gives me confidence to move through all situations, challenges and concerns, knowing I have a buddy!

Whether it's a cup with a delicate handle or a sturdy one, or a Japanese teacup with no handle at all, I thank God for all these ways that He helps us sense hot emotions, and how He guides us in adjusting them via this awareness. Even on the shelf, it can help me take an instant reading of my emotions, and cool them down to balance with Divine Spirit's. Just think of how we can use this "Tea-Handle-Secret" if we get in the middle of an argument; or get annoyed when we're on hold too long on the phone when we're supposed to be receiving "customer service"; or when our children threaten to drive us up the wall when we're tired. Definitely - the teacup's handle is a handy thing!

What Fun, to Look at a Teacup and Know You're Praying!

Over the years, I've taught many classes to busy women (and men), and I've always sought ways to make life easier for them. But when God promised to help me with this Tea Ceremony, I had no idea how easy He would make things! It's enough to make a grown woman giggle, as if she has a secret others would want. (Which is why she shared it!) Not only is my prayer time easier, but now I find it so fun to look at a teacup on the shelf, and know I'm praying! What a hoot! After all, what law said we couldn't have fun in prayer time?

I guess you could say, I have fun in two ways. Number one: I realize this Tea Ceremony process is such a fun way to pray, that I let myself HAVE FUN. I let myself enjoy pretty teacups, a little lace, or a flower. I let myself put my feet up and my worries down - and I do so with a new lightness of being. I say Thank You, God, with a smile on my face!

And number two: I FEEL GOOD about all the answers and enLIGHTenments I've received. No matter how serious the challenges and problems I brought to my prayer time were, I received a lifting of emotions, and inspirations that were surprising! Isn't God great, that He can surprise us so! I for one, am so glad that the Tea Ceremony reminds me to open up, let God take me out of the box of my own thinking - and be continually, deliciously surprised by all I can receive!

The process of Prayer and Tea and Thee is itself a great and splendid surprise, one I was happy to find filled with some much-needed, easy-going delight. Now I look at my teacups and know I'm joining with God in a new way. I'm having FUN.

The Teacup's Mighty Power

"This is just a teacup" some might say - but the people who practice Prayer and Tea and Thee say that no more, for now our teacup is one of our best friends. As we pass by it, our spirit is changed, but we know it's changed for a precise reason. We know that as we look at our teacup, and simply think of our prayers, we're MULTIPLYING THE POWER OF THOSE PRAYERS.

Wow! What an amazing thing to do! What an opportunity! "I can't wait to do it again," you say. And the great thing is you can do it again so easily, now that you've let God into something you use each day. *Where once a decorative teacup sat, now a mighty teacup brightens your prayers, letting you multiply the light within them.* For now you realize, that just as the Tea Ceremony is about more than merely drinking tea, your teacup is a remarkable and inspiring symbol of God's continual presence and loving power within your everyday life.

As you look at the soft butter-yellow cup, you may multiply the energy of healing. As you look at the deep purple cup, you may multiply the happiness in a circle of friends. And as you look at the soft pink roses on a pretty teacup, you may multiply the strength of your dreams. Each teacup will be imbued with your own prayers and meanings, of course, and the beauty is that you get to personalize them, and even let what prayer-meaning that teacup holds for you change over time. New prayers will come your way, but you'll receive them with new confidence, for you have a mighty teacup in your prayer repertoire - and what a multiplier of God's Love that is!

The shape and delicacy of Love.   The flowers of inspiration.   The colors that capture the heartbeat of our prayers - all these incredible gifts come as we glance at a mighty teacup, and feel God's goodwill beaming brightly in our everyday lives.   *A lovely reminder not only of our prayers - but of how constantly and abundantly we are Loved!*

A Bubblebath
For the Spirit!

How the Comfort of Beauty's Ways Helps Your Spirit Luxuriate.

As we've found, hardly a day that goes by that we don't need what we might describe as *a bubblebath for our spirit* - but it might look a little funny if we actually took a bubblebath at work! Or it might be hard to fit in at 10 in the morning, after we're already showered and in the middle of activities. And can we always fit a bubblebath into the middle of a busy evening with family or friends? The possibilities of this exquisite retreat often diminish as rapidly as our need for it increases! For oh so many reasons it's a relief to have the Tea Ceremony at our fingertips, so easy to do - offering the luxurious comfort that feels so divine, it must be a bubblebath for our spirit!

But how do these beautiful bubblebath-for-the-spirit moments help us? Is this a habit we Need or is it just a nice frivolity? It pays us dividends to think about where this lands on our list of priorities, for if we truly understand the importance of beauty's ways, we'll allow ourselves this much-needed "luxury" - not just for a week or two, but for a lifetime. And think what a lifetime of Tea Ceremonies will do for us!

How a Little Beauty Alleviates Our Insanity-Factor!

For most women, it doesn't take long for a day to get complicated with all the *different* kinds of responsibilities we juggle - the "This-and-That's of Life," as I call them. This morning, for instance, I'm thinking a bit about a few financial details; my son's medical appointment; ordering some health supplements; two upcoming birthday celebrations this week; buying another gift (and what it should be!); and how to fit in a visit to the chiropractor and do three loads of laundry - *plus* my own work – all *before* my Schwan's man stops by for my food order. And whoops, I have to call him and say I'll be back late because of the chiropractic appointment! Whoosh, where's the attention to my spirit in all of this? Gone with the wind, if I don't have an easy answer.

If women, or men, react by putting their heads down and pushing through everything on their To Do List, our insanity-factors could escalate just by thinking about it! At this point, we can let our stress factors continue to build, or do something constructive about them. The beauty of the Tea Ceremony is that it quickly decreases our insanity-factor by bringing us comfort *of a different kind.* Different than watching a movie, which helps us relax but doesn't always help us resolve our deepest inner conflicts. Different than eating, which can be comforting but adds unwanted calories. Even different than a conversation with someone, because that conversation may not always bring us peace.

No, the kind of comfort in the Tea Ceremony is a world apart. It is a bubblebath for the spirit, offering us a luxurious soak, a truly refreshing break from the hectic world in a way that relaxes us from the inside, out, meeting our "insanity-factor" at whatever point it is, at any time of the day or night. Now, as we sip our cup of tea, it's important to acknowledge that we need this soul-soothing time of comfort, that even though it feels wonderfully indulgent, *it is a real and vital NEED.*

After all, how different life is if we go through the motions of doing some good deeds, *telling ourselves* we're being of service, when we're really a ball of tension, ready to self-destruct?! Or just busy and tense enough to have a certain edge to our voice? Or overwhelmed enough to drift into a negative mental zone?

If we think we don't need a habit of accepting luxurious loving comfort, we might be totally, totally wrong! In actuality, God needs bright spirits to do the good work of the heart and mind, so He needs us to value our mental health. And one of the best ways to do that is to practice sipping our tea, and to enjoy a heart-warming bubblebath for our spirit, knowing it is a healthy and very vital spiritual need.

The Language of Beauty, in All Its Ways

How is it that beauty helps us? How is it that the bubblebath-for-the-spirit kind of beauty we feel in the Tea Ceremony bolsters our spirit so well? I don't know all the reasons why, but as an artist, I know it does. There have been studies showing that people work better in beautiful rooms rather than disheveled ones, for our environment affects our spirit. That makes sense to me! As I just pointed out, in the course of my morning, my mind can easily become over-loaded, moving from a sense of peace and beauty, to a sense of frenzy and dysfunction that feels as disheveled as an uncared for room. So having a bit of beauty in our lives, such as the beauty and grace of the Tea Ceremony, helps us ease our tension, clear the channels of our minds, and find a place where we can breathe. A place where we can then create - and give again, with Love.

This is the creative place Spirit wants us to reside, so we may flourish rather than merely survive. Indeed, cre-ativity is such a building block in our lives and how we live them, that removing the clutter from our minds is pivotal. We need a clean canvas on which to create. Beauty, in its many ways, can do that. In the Tea Ceremony, beauty can act as a medicine for the spirit, healing us with its gifts of new beginnings. Maybe it's the flowers on a teacup that soften us. Or the grace of hot water flowing into it that calms us, and helps us enter the exquisite here and now. Or the del-icate aroma of the tea itself that infuses our spirit with a feeling of enchantment - of dreams that want to be born.

Beauty tends us in ways known, and in ways barely understood. But unlocking its mysteries is simpler than we think. Unconsciously, our spirit knows what feels right to it, what beauties makes it sing. Our "job" then, is just to listen, so we may understand beauty's language as it pertains to us. So we might answer its request. *What teacup feels beautiful to you? What tea sounds delicious? What area inside your home, or outside upon your deck, calls to your spirit, wanting to share its beauty with you today?*

OK, I'm thinking, this is a "job" I like volunteering for! Beauty, come my way!

Detoxifying Our Inner Environment

As we're now much more aware (since we've been practicing our Tea Ceremony), we have two kinds of environments, both outer - and inner. As a society, we often think of cleaning up our outer environment - we clean up rivers; the beach; and even our house - but as we know, it's just as important to clean up our inner environment. In our Tea Ceremony, we actively take charge of our inner environment when we "Raise Our Teacup, and Raise Our Vibration." As we do, we cleanse our spirit - and our way of thinking - so, step-by-step, sip-by-sip, we can seek to match the Love and creative energy of Divine Spirit's higher vibration instead.

What a relief, and what a healthy thing then, to de-stress, and detoxify our inner environment - and to consciously understand what we're doing! For the mind and heart get toxins thrown at them all too often. It might be the result of a talk with someone that morning. A toxic word is spoken, and you end up dealing with its poison all day long. Or it might be a situation that's stressful, even traffic can quickly sour the spirit. In times like this, what better creative solution than a bubblebath for the spirit to de-stress and detoxify the special environment of our spirit, so we can find our way back to beauty's ways - and let that change the way we live our day. Just remembering the value of cleansing and renewing our spirit is an integral part of the Tea Ceremony, *for it helps build a valuable new habit.*

Making Space for Beautiful Moments in Our Lives

When I step out of a bubblebath, I'm usually a happier person. Warm. Relaxed. Refreshed. When we understand what happens when we immerse ourselves in a bubble-bath-for-our-spirit, we realize *what a worthwhile thing it is to let a little bit of heaven tend us.* What a great thing it is to allow ourselves to find peace in gentle ways, by making space for beautiful moments in our lives. Now when we see our cup of tea, we may think about what a difference a renewed life force makes! One of the biggest changes we'll find in ourselves is dramatic, and can change our life in astounding ways, so it's well worth our acknowledgement. *We may find that we give up the habit of striving and struggling so hard.* We'll still work, of course, but we learn to care for ourselves during the course of our days and weeks.

To let ourselves have the beautiful moments that calm the spirit and soothe the heart.

As we practice this act of gentleness for our spirit, the power of Love in it brings surprises of its own. As it spills over, we often find our whole life is gentler. We're gentler. And we're living at a difference pace - a pace with a rhythm that seems to include us, and so allows for the growth of our spirit within the pulse of our day. This enables us to pray for ourselves and for others in an entirely different way, in a way that is neither rote nor hurried, but is full of sunshine's genuine grace.

What a natural upper it is for us when we make time for the REAL NEEDS of our body, mind and spirit, for when we feel whole and in balance, we resonate with a happiness that changes everything. Now, when we take a sip of tea, we can accept these moments of luxury *without any sense of guilt.* Embracing a healthier way of being, we may now celebrate the difference we see in ourselves when we make space for the beautiful moments, that tend us from the inside, out.

Yes, Teatime is a much-needed time to luxuriate. When we take time to remember we are real people, not super heroes, and this is more than a frivolous desire but a real life Need, we nurture a habit that goes far beyond the world of strife and struggle - and in that moment, we let our world subtly and dramatically transform. *When we're asked what real life blessings and life-giving changes have come from this bubblebath for the spirit?*

Each of us could say, "Let me count the ways!"

Deciding Serenity Isn't Such a "Little Thing"!

Appreciating.

Blue skies of thought. Mountain meadows that offer up surprising wildflowers of new ideas. Chickadees that bounce from branch to branch as if buoyed by the morning's happiness. In some ways, this is one of the best kept secrets: just how GOOD prayer makes us feel! What happens to the heart when Sunshine flows in . . . when tears are finally released and shared with a Friend who truly cares . . . when our whole being comes into alignment with God's positive force within our everyday lives. Wow, it's like visiting the best garden on the best day - full of such awesome potential to tend us in every which-way. No, Serenity isn't such a "little thing" - it's a Girl Friend's (and a Guy Friend's) thing!

A Walk through the Garden, a Cool Kind of Review

Yes, prayer does really make us feel good. It's like walking through a great garden. When you start out, you may not know what to think. Then, as you proceed, you become more and more entranced by the beauty you find there. And when you get into the heart of the garden, you realize you never want to leave! Why? Because it's changed you. One way or another, you've probably been soothed and your spirit has been refreshed. Recharged. Able to take this good feeling out into the rest of your day.

Take a moment to remember how you feel when you leave a wonderful park or garden. Some of my favorite "friends" are the Portland Rose Gardens and the Japanese Garden, happily placed side by side. If you're like me, after your visit, you may be overflowing with images. You can hardly wait to tell someone how beautiful it was, and if they'll listen, you want to give them details:

The flowering Japanese Cherry tree, with soft pink blossoms that cluster like spring bouquets. The winding path of stones that fit together just right. The Trilliums, stunning white blossoms nestled like gifts under Fir trees in the forest. And the row upon row of stunning Roses, heralding Summer's rite, to sit awhile and dream, unfettered by schedules that don't fit the soul's need for fragrance and fresh aire.

To our spirit's delight, the garden of prayer offers the same eloquent gifts, so as we leave our own resplendent garden of prayer, it's fun to do the same thing – and list the beauty we've taken in. It's a cool kind of review!

What did you find in your walk in the garden of prayer today, or this week? What were the stones that fit together just right? What were the soft pink blossoms of insights that now cluster like spring bouquets? Have you talked about them, or written them down? By doing either of these things, we give voice not only to our gratitude, but to all we are receiving. And we begin to see a big thing: how utterly cool prayer is!

This week, for instance, prayer has helped me walk differently. More like I'm in a garden than on the speedway. And this seems to be quite good for both me and for the people around me! I actually talk to the grocery store clerk, and take time to look into her eyes - as if she's a flower to be treasured instead of ignored. And oh, the smiles I get back! This is what some would call an "ordinary" thing, but I find it builds a whole community of friends here. A neighborhood of people who look forward to their everyday exchanges - and that's a big thing.

As my husband reviewed his prayer time, he said it makes him feel closer to God, and as that happens, he "feels less jambled". Wow, how true that is! He added that another big gift from prayer is how he can now "look through" temporary situations, and see the long term view in them.

Ah, that we might walk through the garden of prayer and only glean the things my husband listed. These two alone would be the bounty of a lifetime! But what intrigues me beyond that, is what happens when we share conversations like this. When I really see the garden of inspirations and insights that now exists for us, I see the big difference prayer time makes in my life. As you might guess from the cover of this book, *I look at my teacup today, and see flowers. So many awesome flowers!*

The Big Deal
Is the Feeling Inside Us Now

There's a big feeling inside me now, and as I review prayer time, it's nice to feel that song within me, and give it voice.   The song-filled notes that come are big ones. *Serenity.   Strength.   Bigger spirit.   Confidence.   Love. Wholeness.   Compassion.   Humbleness.   Sheer Joy - just to name a few.*

Where else can you obtain such gifts?! And isn't it wonderful to know that because of an ongoing practice of prayer through the fun and ease of something like the Tea Ceremony, we may receive this garden of bonuses all the time?! The big deal, of course, is that these bonuses are inside us. They walk with us. They bless us - constantly. I could run out of exclamation points, just trying to list the gifts that grace and change our lives. But the added benefit is that listing them actually strengthens them - and what a terrific secret this is! For to actually get our mind around these big changes in our lives is to truly give them power. The big, good kind of power that lifts our lives, and makes us a flower in the garden - so we might also help others.

The Impact Teatime Prayer
Has on Those We Love

As we walk through the garden of prayer, we're definitely changed, but how often do we think about how that change affects others, especially those we care for?   The immediate answer is probably pretty straight forward, and happily so, for when we pray for others, we expand the territory of Love.

Every parent knows how important it is and what an honor it becomes to be able to care for another person, instead of just caring for yourself, and how much it transforms *you* in the process. And every friend knows how good it feels to care for another, and see the difference it can make when your friend no longer feels alone. So when we pray for another person, we honor that great and beautiful bridge. To care for another. And to ask for God's insights, so we might be a sacred conduit of Divine Love's comfort and guidance within someone's life.

Review for just a moment the insights and good old-fashioned help you've received for someone else because of prayer time. Maybe you've received it at the moment of prayer, or the insight walked in afterward when you least expected it. But you knew it when it came into your heart. Maybe your prayer time inspired you to call a particular friend that day - just when she needed it. Or maybe you were gifted with the insight to take your child to a particular doctor, naturopath, or energy worker. Maybe, because of your prayer, a friend conveyed the name of a natural supplement to you - one that would greatly aid your child's healing.

All of these things have happened to me. They just happen more frequently now because of Teatime prayer. And that's a wonderful thing to notice!

But the other way our prayer time affects our loved

ones is in who we become because of prayer. Do all the
things I listed before *(Serenity, Strength, Bigger spirit,
Confidence, Love, Wholeness, Compassion, Humbleness,
Sheer Joy - just to name a few)* increase the gift of who we are
to our loved ones? You bet they do! As we think about it,
they're probably our greatest gifts, and in their own ways,
add to the beautiful garden of our relationship with them.
Think about what a difference Serenity alone can make . . .
What a difference Compassion can make . . . And what a difference our own Wholeness can bring to a friend who needs
our help.

Deciding the Direction We'll Walk

Reviewing the gifts that prayer time brings is not
such a little thing, for we find that Serenity isn't such a little thing. Instead, we see that prayer time is the gateway to
our life, and when we start praying, we open the door to the
garden, and literally start deciding the direction of our life.
Do we want to live in the light? Do we want the gentle honor
of walking beside inspiring flowers? Do we want to feel the
refreshing caress of cascading waterfalls? Do we want to see
the curved path, with stones fitting together, leading us with
a grace that can only be found in the garden?

As we take these short moments of time to review our
life each week, we may see a big thing - that our life is
taking a good direction. And we will know, with a deep sense
of contentedness, that this is no mere accident. That we
decided, at first with a sigh and then with a grin, to put our

feet up and our worries down, and take a Serenity Break for Tea.   When we did, something magical happened. To our continual astonishment and delight, we found ourselves in the garden, in a walk that brings us such blessings . . . *Blue skies of thought. Mountain meadows that offer up surprising wildflowers of new ideas. Chickadees that bounce from branch to branch as if buoyed by the morning's happiness.* To our hearts now, thankfully this is no longer a best-kept secret. As we make our joyful list, it feels wonderful to show our appreciation, and tell God just how GOOD prayer makes us feel!

Teatime

Is Anytime, Anywhere -

Thank Goodness!

Committing to Everyday Magic.

In this early April morning, my white china teacup with the purple pansies fits into my hand like an old friend. This morning, after months and months with the Tea Ceremony, I feel so much more assured, confidant in a new way. For as I sit here in my burgundy chair, I know how easily I can find time to pray. Now I know I have only to lift my cup, and the fun steps of the Tea Ceremony will bring a smile to my face. That this can happen so early in the morning - while I'm still getting my act together - is definitely a sign it works!

Fortunately, the Art of Prayer and Tea and Thee does help me get my act together, subtly changing me where I'm at. I sigh thankfully, like a kid who finally gets a lollipop he or she has been hankering for, knowing that now I no longer have to find "the perfect" time or place to get close to God and be tended in that special way. What a treat!

Everyday Places, for Everyday Magic

Nowadays, magic is everywhere. Sharing our smiles, my friends and I describe some of the places that are sweeter today because we can sip tea, or coffee, or hot chocolate - and easily partake in a dollop of prayer. Amanda loves her big overstuffed chair in the family room at home, and Jessica has found she can even pray at the office. When she takes a work break, any cup, whether china or Styrofoam, will do. As Jessica says, her contemplative "tea-moments" give her a chance to get centered again, and let the warmth of God's Love infuse her spirit, sip by gentle sip.

Now, as her hand slips around an everyday tea or coffee cup, she lets herself reclaim her own private space, and even when she's around other people, finds she has "room to pray". In the process of praying at work, she's found herself praying for people she wouldn't have thought to pray for before, people in need that we might consider "on the periphery" of our lives. Like the receptionist. The sales person. The blind man who operates the snack bar.

"As I've prayed for these people I see everyday, I realize I'd been taking them for granted," Jessica admits. "The act of adding them to my prayer time has unexpectedly blessed me. Now my world has expanded, and something is shared in the process that's magical. Like an invisible road of goodwill has opened up between us - and the road doesn't just go from me to them. God's right in the middle of it, bringing more warmth to me as I do it." Jessica smiles as she continues, "Now I look forward to these unexpected prayers. As I follow God's lead and notice other people, He's opening up my world, as well as my heart. I'm experiencing life differently now. It's as if my world is a bigger and brighter place, *full* of people I care about."

Sometimes the magic that happens, happens *within us* as we take time to pray. Even today I found my own heart expanding yet again as I took Jessica's lead and prayed for the people in the elevator with us at the Veterans Hospital. How good it felt! And how beautiful it is that God keeps giving to us in these unexpected ways! In so many ways, God seeks to help us and *all* the ones we care for . . .

From 2 Minutes to 10 — You Can Help Change the World

As I set down my paperwork, I pick up my ivory coffee cup I purchased on a great trip to the coast, knowing that anytime, anywhere now, I can partake of tea. What a comfort it is, for on some days I have plenty on my mind. But here, in the middle of my day at my round dining room table overlooking my garden, I know it's so attainable. This art of prayer is a gift that helps change the way I look at things, and that seems to change everything. I know now, even in 2 minutes or in 10, I can help change the world, *by changing my inner world first.*

How often, when I lift my teacup, do I realize I've been worrying rather than praying! But, because of the Tea Ceremony, that knowledge creates an instant shift. Now, it's almost like snapping my fingers. *"Snap out of it!"* we might say, as we laugh at ourselves - or *"Snap into it!* Get back into Higher Territory! Start enjoying a fine conversation with God instead."

Ah, the luxury of it. To see how Higher Spirit views things. It doesn't take that long to make this slight shift, and enter the territory of Love and Wisdom that waits at our fingertips - literally at our fingertips when we reach for our teacup! Now we've become like Olympic athletes in a way; we've trained ourselves - our body, mind and spirit - to turn toward God. I like this kind of practice, especially for what it does for me. The *results* are Olympic!

In 2 to 10 minutes, I can calm down. I can breathe new life into my brain - and into my spirit. And I can gain wisdom's edge. This is a positive edge. A powerful place where new ideas and ways of proceeding are brought to our doorstep, are kindly and profoundly placed there for us to receive. This alone has changed me, has changed the next steps I take in any problem I face or my loved ones face, and has changed the timetable within which I act. Sometimes the higher guidance I receive is to wait, rather than to act - which has surprised me but has also given me the bonus of newfound, and well-founded, patience. It feels much better now to calmly wait rather than pace!

My friends report their own changes, also. John found the short but consistent tea breaks he now calls his "best-friend-time" helped him walk through his father's illness, what John was told in prayer time would be his father's long walk home. Considering John's often irritable and emotionally distant father, this was not an easy thing to do, but because of prayer, John made time in his busy life, made seeing his father even more of a priority than before, and let compassion soften his heart toward his father. They became closer in a hard-to-describe, ethereal way. Way beyond the everyday expectations we all get caught in. Way beyond memories of the past.

As John tended his father in this new way, John saw how it was helping his dad, but what he didn't expect was something else that happened. John liked the person he became in the process. As he practiced compassion with his dad, John says he suddenly felt freer and more loving. With a new sense of ease, he looked at other people more compassionately, and found himself connecting on a different level. Now he didn't want to give up this new part of himself. Along the way, something magical had happened. His world had changed.

One of the Biggest Changes: Your Spirit's Radiating Joy

At the moment I write this, the CD on my stereo is switching from some slower, soothing piano music to some lilting Celtic songs. I can feel God laughing with me, as I see how it reflects so perfectly just what wants to be conveyed: how, after we are soothed and healed in prayer time, this beautiful, lilting Joy comes radiating out of us. Into the world. Changing things just by its being!

Such an awesome Joy it is, it's hard to describe, but it's important to let ourselves feel it. Yes, life is full of its challenges. Plenty of them. And we can get bogged down in them, and end up thinking prayer time is just that - a time to be bogged down in our problems. But at the end of each of my Prayer and Tea and Thee workshops, people are pretty much radiating! Each of us usually arrives a little laden with our everyday stresses, but I can see that lift so naturally as we proceed through the Tea Ceremony. It's like watching the sunshine come out after a spring shower - soon you expect it as the most natural of occurrences!

Accepting the bonus of Peace and Joy that comes through prayer time is another step in the art of Prayer and Tea and Thee. But we were meant to practice this joyful acceptance, for Inner Peace is a radiant thing, a gift that offers the people around us shelter, comfort, and confidence. It's simply wonderful to be in a roomful of people after a Prayer and Tea and Thee workshop! We're all just ordinary folks - folks who have been magically changed by the power and grace of the Love we now feel within us. Smiles are exchanged. People chatter like birds on the line. And a relaxed Joy seems to permeate the room.

It changes me just to be in this happy environment. And the Joy I feel from it stays with me. I can recall it in an instant, and as I do, it always changes me. This is the powerful gift that flows through us, so ready to affect others in the same way. It's not a little thing - but a life-changer.

Being Present to Care.
Being Present to Heal.
Being Present to Accept Love.

The power of Wisdom and Joy that wells up from our conversations with God is also the very source of our Healings, large and small - so great is the power of its positive energy! When we pray and let the thunderbolt of God's Love flow through us, we can affect our own lives and the lives of others. But it always begins by being present. Being present to care. For then we can be present to heal.

How do we do that? By being present to accept God's Love. And through God's direction, to let it flow into all things. Into the body, mind and spirit. Into situations and into stumbling blocks of fears we can barely see. Whether in ourselves, or in those we care about, there are places Love yearns to flow. It is one of the greatest Joys in life, to be there. To be present to let Love flow. To ask, and have the honor of listening - and receiving.

Sometimes we'll hear words. Sometimes we'll receive a feeling. And sometimes an inspiration. And also, sometimes we'll feel the radiating Light of Love flow through our heart and hands, into the place that wants to be healed in someone we care for. Indeed, it is not such a little thing to pray. In so many ways, it changes us, and leads us day by day in the powerful walk of our service.

Teatime Prayer,
a Gift that Keeps on Giving . . .

To lift our teacup.   To enter into the garden of prayer. And then to receive a gift that keeps on giving - how beyond anything we could have asked for is this!   Now, to walk with this greater Lightness of Being is one of our greatest Joys. It's a gift we know we can have in the morning, even when the dew is still on the ground. Or in the afternoon, when we think we've lost our footing. Or in the evening, when we especially need the bright night stars around us. The knowledge that anytime, anywhere, God's comfort and guidance is with us - in every step of our walk - brings a sustenance and Joy that is beyond measure. A gift we can hardly comprehend, even as we are asked to accept it.

Learning to live like this, in the presence of such Peace and Joy, helps us extend beyond the borders of who we thought we were, and become who we were intended to be. All of us were meant to be a blessing to others. To find and use our gifts. And to help others do the same. We were meant to find our angel's wings, and in the Prayer and Tea and Thee workshops, I see many! Beautiful women and men who seek to make a difference, who care about their time of prayer, and who decide to receive that luminous gift of God's Love and Peace. Then let it radiate out, into their everyday lives.

How much more beautiful could it be?

Thank you, God, for this gift that keeps on Giving. And for all the people who lift their cups of tea, and let your warm thunderbolt of Love flow through them. *Sip by sip, we feel you transforming our hearts. Changing our world. Day by day, we feel those good ol' kind of tears, as we feel you filling our cups with your beautiful flowers of Love.*

We promise you one sweet and easy thing: *we'll keep on practicing.*

Part IV:

Ceremony

Remembrance Poem

*After writing this book, I still wanted something short
and simple to instantly remind us of the steps in the
PRAYER & TEA & THEE™ Ceremony. The answer
that came? To my relief and delight, not the usual 1-2-3 list,
but instead this lyrical prayer-poem.*

*Every time we read it, may it bless our hearts, and
remind each of us of the incredible Circle of Love
we share.*

May you have many beautiful teatime moments,

Sheila

"A Teatime Prayer"

Sheila Stephens

Dear God, please
lead me into Comfort's Ways.
Let me bring you the cup
of who I am,
which you find special
everyday.
Help me open to your Grace
as I sit awhile,
comfortable enough to say,
"I put my feet up now,
and set my worries down -
into your hands today."

Let me remember,
in these moments of
much-needed ease,
the many ways you've tended me,
and filled my cup
with the splendid blessings
you so constantly
send my way.

Help me merge with you,
as I steep my tea
and center myself –
to receive your Love-filled Light.
And when that sip of warmth
spreads through me,
let it heal all the places in my spirit
that were in need.

As I feel that healing Light,
as I surrender to you
my worry and my pain -
cleanse my heart
and comfort my emotions,
so I may regain my sacred balance -
in the centerpoint
and steadfast warmth
of your fine Love.

And as this gentle teatime
renews the all of me,
let me lift my teacup,
and my prayers,
into the wings of your
higher Vibration,
so I may let your radiant energy
imbue my every thought
with Vision, with Wisdom,
and with the Guidance
of your luminous Insight.

I promise, dear God, to honor
the rich servings of blessings
and inspirations
you so generously
bring to me – by using them
in my life today.
And I promise
to come back to you often –
so you may see me smiling
when I hear the clink of fine china,
or nodding
when I see a teacup on a shelf –
knowing that this day
and this prayer
are not mine alone,
but shared with You.

Thank you, God,
for this teatime,
and for the gift of Love
you ever bring my way.
I go forth now,
with you in my Heart,
as I let you fill
and change my day
with the warmth and radiance
of your Grace.

"A Teatime Prayer"
© 2004, Sheila Stephens
A complimentary on-line copy of this poem
is available at Flowers of the Spirit.com

Angels, Birds & Gratitudes . . .

The person I most want to thank is my husband, Allen. His indomitable spirit is so full of love for me and our family that I felt impelled to bloom under his tender-loving care. He put his own Western Fiction ("Gone to Glory" and "Trail of Trouble") aside while he helped me complete a book that we both feel is one of "our" most important works. A work of love.

He often cooked for me, edited, offered brilliant and wise conversations, and even sang rock songs to me when I needed a boost to work through a concept or a paragraph. Most of all he made me smile and feel God's goodness and direction.

Just one year ago (today!), we moved into our new home in Sherwood, and I had much to do that didn't involve writing a book. But after the essentials were in place, I sat down to pray, and asked God what He wanted me to do next with my life. It was at that point God asked me to share *The Art of Prayer & Tea & Thee* – for the rest of my life.

And I agreed. I happily went about finishing a book that sprang from a workshop offered at the OASIS Institute. Many thanks to the wonderful group of "angels" in my workshop. Their friendly, warm-hearted natures inspire me each time I give the Tea Ceremony or write about it.

But I couldn't continue on without thanking Cathy Walter Robb, who inspires everyone at OASIS. With a touch as light as a bird, Cathy encourages creative projects to be born in all of us, as if it's second nature. Thanks also here to my dear friend, Peggy Maduff, who listened to her angels, and suggested going to OASIS at the same time I'd felt the desire to teach there.

These gratitudes wouldn't be complete without thanking my sunshine son, Jim. He has a way of understanding and caring for me that makes me feel so at peace. His compassionate and kind heart is in these pages, and I thank him also for listening to chapters, even before having coffee! I'm also appreciative to my stepson, Julian, who voiced his enthusiasm from Seattle. These two young men let me know I'm loved for who I am, and celebrate whenever I use my gifts.

Another "angel" waited for me in Sherwood. After I moved here I "knew" I'd bump into my dear friend Kathie Liden, and sure enough, I did. Thank you, Kathie for being a mentor, a real friend, and a beacon. Your love and devotion have helped give *Prayer & Tea & Thee* its wings. I am deeply – and forever – touched. You are my teacup of Blessings!

In the same way, Kay Allenbaugh has given me the courage to lovingly lead, and have fun sharing life's powerful insights along the way. Plus, thanks for sharing your healing cat with me, Kay!

My life wouldn't be the same without these people, including ones like Lisa Robertson, who proofed the manuscript, but added so much to my writing classes by her presence, that I just love being around her.

Also, thanks to my caring mom and all the prayers and girl friend teatimes we have around the kitchen table, and the wealth of family and friends. Even though I haven't met all the people Allen knows in Hillsboro who cheer us on, your faith is part of this book project. I look forward to meeting you! Thanks to the fun people at TOPS, Willamette Writers, the friendly librarians at the Tigard Library, and retired volunteer coordinator, Jean Lindsay. It was Jean who helped me start teaching, and it's these inspiring students (and friends) who make it so rewarding.

Thank you, foremost, to God, who helps us with our gifts, imbuing them with a purpose that teaches us, softens us, and strengthens us – in ways beyond our understanding. In ways that stir the birds to fly with joy on their wings – knowing they were meant to do so.

– Sheila Stephens

Visit

Flowers of the Spirit.com

Books, fun Workshops & Gifts
reflecting

Love ❤ *Light* ❤ *Life!*

Featuring works by Sheila Stephens:

❤ The Art of Prayer & Tea & Thee

❤ Walking With the Flowers

❤ Adventures in Writing 101

❤ FREE e-newletter

❤ COMPLIMENTARY on-line copy of

  "A Teatime Prayer"

FlowersOfTheSpirit.com

Share the fun of Teatime Moments With Your Favorite People!

- ❤ Girl Friends
- ❤ Sisters
- ❤ Woman's Group
- ❤ Moms, Daughters
- ❤ Grandmothers
- ❤ Prayer Group

A Perfect Choice for

- ❤ Fundraising
- ❤ Birthdays
- ❤ Mother's Day
- ❤ Prayer Day
- ❤ Volunteer Gifts
- ❤ Thank-You
- ❤ Holiday Gifts
- ❤ Secret Pal

"The Art of Prayer & Tea & Thee"

<u>Price:</u>   <u>Shpg & Hdlg:</u>   Prices valid only

$14.95/book $3.00/book   in continental USA

100% moneyback guarantee, if returned in new condition,
up to 6 months after purchase (5 book limit on returns).

(Please fax request for additional volume and fundraising discounts to: (503) 925-8564, or visit Web Site, FlowersOfTheSpirit.com)

Note: All prices are subject to change.

Date: _____

Name: _____

Address: _____

City & Zip: _____

Phone #: _____

Confirmation e-mail: _____

PLEASE SEND ME:

The Art of Prayer & Tea & Thee

_____ copies @ $14.95/each = ——————

shpg & hdlg @ $3/each = ——————

TOTAL DUE: ——————

*Please send your check or money order to:

Flowers of the Spirit LLC

PO Box 1028 / Sherwood, OR 97140

Flowers
of the Spirit™

"because each of us
is a Flower of the Spirit"